The 25 Rules to

MW01202035

About the Book

Grammar & Punctuation includes:

25 Rule Charts

Use the charts to introduce the rules. Choose the rules and the order of use that is appropriate to your students' needs.

Student Practice Pages

Each rule is supported by 3 scaffolded, reproducible practice pages. Use the level that is appropriate for your students. The pages may be used with the whole class or as independent practice. They are also useful as homework review.

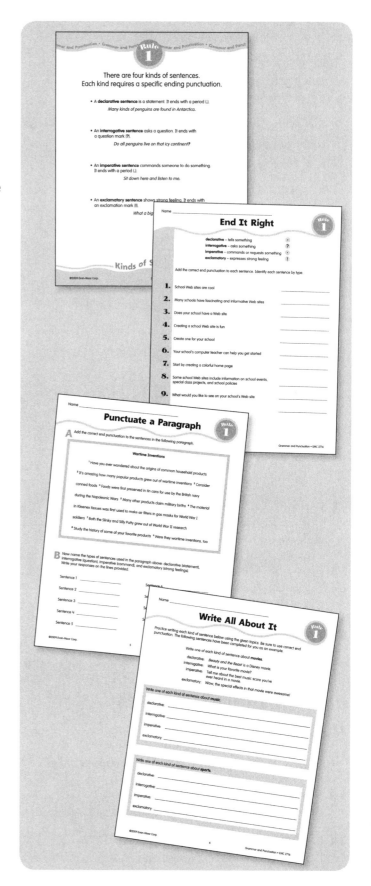

Rule 1

There are four kinds of sentences. Each kind requires a specific ending punctuation.

- A **declarative sentence** is a statement. It ends with a period (.).

  Many kinds of penguins are found in Antarctica.

- An **interrogative sentence** asks a question. It ends with a question mark (**?**).

  Do all penguins live on that icy continent?

- An **imperative sentence** commands someone to do something. It ends with a period (.).

  Sit down here and listen to me.

- An **exclamatory sentence** shows strong feeling. It ends with an exclamation mark (**!**).

  What a big surprise!

Kinds of Sentences

End It Right

declarative – tells something   •

interrogative – asks something   ?

imperative – commands or requests something   •

exclamatory – expresses strong feeling   !

Add the correct end punctuation to each sentence. Identify each sentence by type.

1. School websites are cool   _____

2. Many schools have fascinating and informative websites   _____

3. Does your school have a website   _____

4. Creating a school website is fun   _____

5. Create one for your school   _____

6. Your school's computer teacher can help you get started   _____

7. Start by creating a colorful home page   _____

8. Some school websites include information on school events, special class projects, and school policies   _____

9. What would you like to see on your school's website   _____

10. Make it happen   _____

Name _____

Punctuate a Paragraph

A Add the correct end punctuation to the sentences in the following paragraph.

Wartime Inventions

[1] Have you ever wondered about the origins of common household products

[2] It's amazing how many popular products grew out of wartime inventions [3] Consider

canned foods [4] Foods were first preserved in tin cans for use by the British navy

during the Napoleonic Wars [5] Many other products claim military births [6] The material

in Kleenex tissues was first used to make air filters in gas masks for World War I

soldiers [7] Both the Slinky and Silly Putty grew out of World War II research

[8] Study the history of some of your favorite products [9] Were they wartime inventions, too

---

B Now name the types of sentences used in the paragraph above: declarative (statement), interrogative (question), imperative (command), and exclamatory (strong feelings). Write your responses on the lines provided.

Sentence 1 _____   Sentence 6 _____

Sentence 2 _____   Sentence 7 _____

Sentence 3 _____   Sentence 8 _____

Sentence 4 _____   Sentence 9 _____

Sentence 5 _____

Name _____

Write All About It

Rule
1

Practice writing each kind of sentence below using the given topics. Be sure to use correct end punctuation. The following sentences have been completed for you as an example.

Write one of each kind of sentence about **movies**.

declarative:	*Beauty and the Beast* is a Disney movie.
interrogative:	What is your favorite movie?
imperative:	Tell me about the best music score you've ever heard in a movie.
exclamatory:	Wow, the special effects in that movie were awesome!

Write one of each kind of sentence about **music**.

declarative: _____

interrogative: _____

imperative: _____

exclamatory: _____

Write one of each kind of sentence about **sports**.

declarative: _____

interrogative: _____

imperative: _____

exclamatory: _____

2

Every complete sentence has a subject and a predicate.

- **Subject**—names the person, place, or thing the sentence is about.

  The **complete subject** contains all the words that tell who or what the sentence is about.

  The **simple subject** is the main noun or pronoun in the subject.

  simple subject

  Our crazy dog howled at the wind.

  complete subject

- **Predicate**—tells what the subject is or does.

  The **complete predicate** contains all the words that tell what the subject is or does.

  The **simple predicate** is the verb of the sentence.

  simple predicate

  Eric and Marshall raced down the street.

  complete predicate

Subjects & Predicates

Find the Subject

Underline the complete subject in each sentence. Circle the simple subject in each sentence.

1. My best friend lives in Thailand.

2. Her name is Roongthip.

3. Roongthip's name means "Rainbow" in Thai.

4. Roongthip's culture is different from mine.

5. Thai money looks different from United States money.

6. The Thai language uses a different alphabet.

7. Thai foods use different spices from those I am used to.

8. Thai cities are filled with intricate architecture.

9. Roongthip's world is different from mine.

10. My friend and I love learning about each other's cultures.

Find the Predicate

Underline the complete predicate in each sentence. Circle the simple predicate in each sentence.

1. My school offers many extra clubs and classes.

2. My brother plays chess with the chess club.

3. My friend Sam plays baseball.

4. I sing with the school choir.

5. Members of the Community Service Club visit elderly people who live alone.

6. They also pick up litter around our town.

7. Members of the journalism class write our school newspaper.

8. The school marching band marches in parades.

9. The pep band plays at football games.

10. Everyone participates in something special at our school.

Sentence or Not?

Decide whether each group of words below is a complete sentence. If the group of words is a complete sentence, capitalize the first letter of the first word and add the correct end punctuation. If the group of words is not a complete sentence, add a subject or predicate to create a complete sentence using the group of words presented.

1. living in Texas

_____

2. karen is going to Disneyland this summer

_____

3. i love strawberries

_____

4. my uncle and my cousins

_____

5. fifteen students from Mr. Fitch's class

_____

6. write poetry and sing songs

_____

7. plays computer games after school

_____

8. the greatest country in the world

_____

9. he's lost

_____

10. it's basketball season

_____

Rule 3

A compound sentence is made by putting together two or more simple sentences containing related information.

- The parts are usually joined by a conjunction such as **and**, **or**, or **but**.*
- A comma is placed before the conjunction.

Simple sentences:

It began to rain.

Our field trip was canceled.

Compound sentence:

*It began to rain, **and** our field trip was canceled.*

Simple sentences:

I have been studying the spelling words every night.

I expect to get a good grade on the test Friday.

Compound sentence:

*I have been studying the spelling words every night, **and** I expect to get a good grade on the test Friday.*

*See Notes to the Teacher on page 103 for additional information.

Compound Sentences

Study Compound Sentences

Underline the complete subject once and the complete predicate twice in **each part** of the compound sentences. Circle the conjunction in each sentence.

1. Movies are exciting, but books are better.

2. I like summer vacation, yet I am always glad when school starts again.

3. We enjoy the beautiful sights in San Francisco, so we chose to vacation in that city.

4. I went to the bank, and then I did my shopping.

5. Art museums are fun to visit, but you need to be prepared to spend the day in them.

6. Beautiful flowers blossom, and then they fade away.

7. Race dogs are fast, but racehorses are faster.

8. English class is hard for me, but math class is easy.

9. Frightening tornadoes destroy property, and earthquakes are devastating, too.

10. Martha and Jerry will go to the beach today, or they will watch a movie.

Name _____

Create Compound Sentences

Rule 3

Use conjunctions to combine each pair of simple sentences into a compound sentence. Place a comma before each conjunction.

1. I love hamburgers. I hate hot dogs.

_____

_____

2. I may go to Mexico this summer. I may go to France.

_____

_____

3. After school I'm going shopping. I'm going to buy a new backpack.

_____

_____

4. Christmas is my favorite holiday. I also enjoy Thanksgiving.

_____

_____

5. Your birthday is on Monday. We'll celebrate this Sunday afternoon.

_____

_____

6. The Little Mermaid is a great book. The Frog Prince is even better.

_____

_____

Simple or Compound?

Sometimes conjunctions appear in simple sentences. Decide whether each of the sentences is simple or compound. Circle your response. Remember, compound sentences contain two simple sentences connected by a conjunction.

1. In his lifetime, Jefferson Davis worked both for and against the United States of America.　　　　simple　　　compound

2. He served in the army and as a congressman, senator, and secretary of war.　　　　simple　　　compound

3. As a senator, Jefferson Davis spoke in favor of slavery and states' rights, but he did not support the idea of secession from the Union.　　　　simple　　　compound

4. Then his home state of Mississippi seceded, and he resigned his position as senator.　　　　simple　　　compound

5. He ordered the South's attack on Fort Sumter, and he became president of the Confederate States of America.　　　　simple　　　compound

6. He was elected for a six-year term, but he was not popular with many of the people who voted for him.　　　　simple　　　compound

7. His leadership and his war tactics were questioned.　　　　simple　　　compound

8. In 1865, Jefferson Davis was captured and imprisoned.　　　　simple　　　compound

9. Eventually, he was indicted for treason, but the United States government dropped the charges.　　　　simple　　　compound

Rule 4

A noun names a person, place, thing, or idea.

- A **common noun** names any person, place, thing, or idea.

    relative   country   boat   freedom

- A **proper noun** names a specific person, place, thing, or idea. A proper noun begins with a capital letter.

    Uncle Elton   New Zealand   Bill of Rights

- **Singular nouns** name one person, place, thing, or idea.

    runner   city   bear   happiness

- **Plural nouns** name more than one.

    workers   schools   horses

Common & Proper, Singular & Plural Nouns

Define the Nouns

Rule
4

Decide whether each of the nouns below is proper or common and plural or singular.
Circle your responses.

1. women   **proper / common**   **plural / singular**

2. Canada   **proper / common**   **plural / singular**

3. universities   **proper / common**   **plural / singular**

4. Butte Falls   **proper / common**   **plural / singular**

5. Dr. Jones   **proper / common**   **plural / singular**

6. libraries   **proper / common**   **plural / singular**

7. Neptune   **proper / common**   **plural / singular**

8. city   **proper / common**   **plural / singular**

9. mice   **proper / common**   **plural / singular**

10. Mickey Mouse   **proper / common**   **plural / singular**

11. books   **proper / common**   **plural / singular**

12. Al Daniels   **proper / common**   **plural / singular**

Capitalize Properly

Write all the proper nouns from the sentences. Remember to capitalize each proper noun.

1. Doris cooksey works for the american family insurance company.

_____

2. Her office is in denver, colorado.

_____

3. Because she lives in bailey, colorado, she commutes to work.

_____

4. Doris drives a honda accord to work each day.

_____

5. She picks up her co-workers dennis, francisco, and ramona along the way.

_____

6. From the train station, the commuters take peterson street to reach their office.

_____

7. For lunch, doris and her friends often walk to the nearby burger hut.

_____

8. Francisco and dennis always order a mega burger.

_____

9. Doris and ramona usually eat salads.

_____

10. Doris and her co-workers enjoy their jobs in denver and their homes in bailey.

_____

Locate the Nouns

Underline all the nouns in the sentences below. Then rewrite the proper nouns on the lines. Be sure to capitalize the proper nouns. Some sentences may contain no proper nouns.

1. Tobias and nolan like to listen to the oldies.

_____

2. Nolan's favorite group is the beach boys.

_____

3. Tobias likes simon and garfunkel.

_____

4. The boys like to watch old movies, too.

_____

5. Nolan's favorite actor is james stewart.

_____

6. Tobias likes to watch joan crawford movies.

_____

7. Nolan and tobias like to visit old ghost towns.

_____

8. They also like to play old card games such as old maid and go fish.

_____

9. The boys' favorite books are all classics such as the adventures of tom sawyer.

_____

10. Maybe tobias and nolan will be historians when they grow up.

_____

Rule 5

Use these rules to make plural nouns.

- To make the plural of most nouns, add **s**.   *automobile**s***

- If a noun ends in *s*, *sh*, *ch*, *x*, or *z*, add **es**.   *bench**es***

- If a noun ends in a consonant followed by a *y*,   *berr**ies***
  change **y** to **i** and add **es**.

- If a noun ends in *f* or *fe*,
  add **s** to some;   *chief**s***
  change **f** to **v** and add **es** to others.   *loa**ves***

- Some nouns do not change when they become plural.

  deer   sheep   moose   salmon

- Some nouns have irregular plural forms.

singular	plural
child	children
goose	geese
mouse	mice
tooth	teeth
ox	oxen

Plural Noun Forms

Regular Plural Nouns

Rule
5

Complete the paragraph using the plural forms for the missing nouns.

Michaela and her mother shopped at three _____ on Christmas Eve.
(store)

At the first stop, they bought six Christmas _____. Their six _____
(gift)   (box)

took up two shopping _____. At the next stop, Michaela looked at a set of
(cart)

_____ for her bedroom, but she didn't buy them. In front of the third store,
(shelf)

Michaela and her mother sat on two _____ to rest. Two _____ with
(bench)   (lady)

_____ sat beside them. Finally, Michaela and her mother made their last stop.
(baby)

They went into the toy store to buy a barrel of _____ for Michaela's little brother.
(block)

At last, Michaela and her mother went home to wrap their _____ and bake
(present)

Christmas _____ before the big holiday.
(goody)

Name _____

Irregular Plurals

Rule
5

A Write the plural form of these words that do not follow the common rules of making plurals. You may use a dictionary to help you.

Plural Form   **Plural Form**

1. deer _____   7. woman _____

2. moose _____   8. man _____

3. person _____   9. sheep _____

4. cactus _____   10. axis _____

5. hypothesis _____   11. series _____

6. crisis _____   12. foot _____

B Now make up nouns of your own to name the five items listed below. Invent the singular and plural form of each new word. Circle *regular* if your new plural noun is regular or *irregular* if it is irregular.

	I'll call it a…	The plural form will be…	
1. an underwater roller coaster	_____	_____	regular irregular
2. a newly discovered breed of fish	_____	_____	regular irregular
3. a new food	_____	_____	regular irregular
4. a type of rock on Mars	_____	_____	regular irregular
5. a coin worth five dollars	_____	_____	regular irregular

Put Plurals Together

Write sentences using the plural forms of the following words.

1. party   cake

_____

2. cow   calf

_____

3. wish   belief

_____

4. strawberry   patch

_____

5. series   game

_____

6. rule   policy

_____

7. dentist   tooth

_____

8. duck   goose

_____

9. man   woman

_____

10. foot   child

_____

Rule 6

A verb is a word in the predicate that tells physical or mental action or a state of being.

- There are three kinds of verbs:

Action verbs tell what the subject is doing.	*We **played** until it was dark.* *Everyone **laughed** at the funny movie.*
Linking verbs link a subject to a noun or an adjective that names or describes it.	*Their dog **is** a Saint Bernard.* *The buttered popcorn **smells** delicious.*
Helping verbs come before the main verb. Helping verbs help state the action or show time.	*Arnold **will** paint the door tomorrow.* *He **has been** painting the frame today.*

- The verb in a sentence must agree in number with the subject.

    If the subject is singular, the verb must be singular.

    > *Iced **lemonade is** refreshing on a hot day.*

    If the subject is plural, the verb must be plural.

    > *Apple **pies are** delicious with vanilla ice cream.*

Verbs

Identify Verb Types

Circle all the action verbs in the sentences. Underline all the linking verbs. Draw a box around all the helping verbs.

1. Mrs. Baker is forty-two years old.

2. She works at an automobile manufacturing plant in Michigan.

3. She has been working there for twenty years.

4. In twenty more years, she will retire.

5. Mr. Baker was forty-two years old last year.

6. He is a year older than Mrs. Baker.

7. He is a librarian at a school library.

8. He finds books for students.

9. He has been helping students for fifteen years.

10. He likes his job.

11. He will work in the library for twenty more years.

12. Then he and Mrs. Baker will travel around the country.

Linking or Action?

Some verbs can be used as either a linking or an action verb. Decide how the verbs in the sentences below are used. Circle your responses.

*Tom **smells** apple pie.*   (action)   linking

*The apple pie **smells** good.*   action   (linking)

1. Bill **feels** uncomfortable giving speeches.   action   (linking)

Martha **feels** the fur on her new bunny.   (action)   linking

2. Karena **looked** for her lost book all morning.   (action)   linking

Terri **looked** happy at her birthday party.   (action)   linking

3. Sandy **turned** the corner at Fifth Street.   action   (linking)

The weather **turned** stormy in the afternoon.   action   (linking)

4. The magician made the coin **appear** behind my ear.   action   linking

The dogs at the show **appear** smart.   action   linking

5. It **grew** quiet in the house after the kids went to bed.   action   linking

Samantha **grew** two inches last summer.   action   linking

6. The tacos at the restaurant **tasted** good.   action   linking

Kim **tasted** the cookie dough before baking the cookies.   action   linking

Subject-Verb Agreement

Circle the verb in each sentence that agrees in number with the subject.

1. Thanksgiving (has   have) always been my favorite holiday.

2. My entire family (get   gets) together on Thanksgiving.

3. We all (enjoys   enjoy) a huge feast.

4. Aunt Mary (bring   brings) the hot rolls.

5. Grandma and Grandpa (bake   bakes) the pumpkin pies.

6. My cousin Tony always (gives   give) me his cranberry sauce.

7. He (let   lets) my brother eat his applesauce.

8. Sauces (is   are) not Tony's favorite part of the meal.

9. My aunts (takes   take) turns washing dishes after dinner.

10. Then the whole gang (play   plays) games for hours.

11. Tony and my brother (likes   like) to play chess.

12. I always (plays   play) cards with my aunts and uncles.

13. Mom and Dad usually (throw   throws) darts.

14. Everyone (find   finds) something fun to do.

15. My family never (want   wants) to go home on Thanksgiving.

Rule 7

The tense of a verb tells when an action occurs— present, past, or future.

- **present**—the action is happening now.

   *Mieko **is practicing** the piano.*

- **past**—the action already happened.

   *She **played** for her teacher yesterday.*

- **future**—the action is going to happen.

   *She **will give** a concert when she learns three more pieces.*

Verb Tenses

When Did It Happen?

Rule
7

Underline the verb or verb phrase in each sentence below. Write the tense of the underlined verb on the line.

Verb Tense

1. A. A. Milne lived from 1882 until 1956.   _____

2. He was an author of plays, essays, short stories, and adult and children's fiction.   _____

3. Milne is remembered for his characterization of Winnie the Pooh.   _____

4. Pooh and his friends Tigger, Eeyore, and Piglet are loved by children and adults alike.   _____

5. Winnie the Pooh stories are classics.   _____

6. They will continue to be popular in the future.   _____

7. Judy Blume is another author who writes for both children and adults.   _____

8. Her children's stories are known more than her adult novels.   _____

9. *Tales of a Fourth Grade Nothing* was written in 1972.   _____

10. It was very popular when it first came out.   _____

11. It is still popular today.   _____

12. People will call it a classic in the future.   _____

Tense Writing

Use context clues to help you select the correct verb tense in these sentences.

1. Mr. Parker (worked   works) in a bank for forty years before he retired last month.

2. Now he (hopes   will hope) to catch up on his woodworking projects.

3. He (has   will have) always liked to build furniture.

4. For his son's birthday in three months, he (hopes   hoped) to have a bookshelf built.

5. He (builds   built) his son a desk for his last birthday.

6. He will have more time to work on this year's gift since he (has   had) retired.

7. School (did   will) let out for summer in six weeks.

8. Then kids in the neighborhood (will spend   are spending) their time at the town's swimming pool.

9. Every year the pool (is   was) especially crowded on the first day of summer.

10. Kevin (moved   moves) to the neighborhood three months ago.

11. He (has   will have) never been to the pool before.

12. He (hopes   hoped) to swim often this summer with his new friends.

Name _____

Locate the Verbs

Underline the verbs in the paragraphs below. Write a **P** above the verb if it happened in the past. Write **PR** above the verb if it is happening in the present. Write an **F** above the verb if it will happen in the future.

Thomas loves to play the piano. He took his first lesson at the age of five. He practices for an hour each day. He especially likes to play classical music. He first heard classical music when he began his lessons. At a concert tomorrow night, he will play his favorite piece, Mozart's "Allegro." The audience will enjoy the concert because Thomas is an excellent pianist.

Stacy is in her town's parade every July. Last year she marched with her school band. This year she is riding her horse. Next year she will find something else to do because she loves to be a part of the parade.

Dana is organizing a talent show at her school. She invited her brother to emcee the event. She asked five of her teachers to judge the show. Now she is getting her friends to sign up for different acts. So far, people have signed up for three singing acts, one comedy performance, and two dancing routines. There will be more sign-ups before the night of the show. Audience and performers alike will have a great time at the show!

Rule 8

Endings are added to verbs to change the tense.

Present

- add **s** to most verbs*   *plays*
- add **ing** and use a present tense helping verb   *is playing*
- verbs ending in *s, ch, sh, x,* or *z*—add **es**   *watches*
- verbs ending in *y*—change **y** to **i** and add **es**   *marries*

Past

- add **ed** to most verbs   *planted*
- add **ed** and use a past tense helping verb   *was planted*
- verbs ending in a single vowel and consonant—   *planned*
  double the final consonant and add **ed**
- verbs ending in *e*—drop the **e** and add **ed**   *raced*
- verbs ending in *y*—change **y** to **i** and add **ed**   *buried*

Future

- use the main verb with **will** or **shall**   ***will** perform*

                                                                              ***shall** visit*

Irregular verbs do not follow a set rule to form the past tense.

eat	ate	give	gave
write	wrote	sing	sang
bring	brought	know	knew
buy	bought	say	said

*See Notes to the Teacher on page 103 for additional information.

Forming Verb Tenses

Name _____

Regular Verb Tense Changes

Rule 8

Rules for changing the tenses of verbs are listed below. After each verb is an example. Provide one more example that follows each rule.

Present Tense Rules   Example

1. Add *s* to most verbs.   sits   _____

2. Add *ing* and use a present tense helping verb.   is eating   _____

3. Add *es* to verbs ending in *s*, *ch*, *sh*, *x*, or *z*.   wishes   _____

4. Change the *y* to *i* and add *es* to verbs ending in *y*. tries   _____

Past Tense Rules

1. Add *ed* to most verbs.   rocked   _____

2. Add *ed* and use a past tense helping verb.   had talked   _____

3. Double the consonant and add *ed* to verbs
   ending in a single vowel and consonant.   trotted   _____

4. Drop the *e* and add *ed* to verbs ending in *e*.   lied   _____

5. Change the *y* to *i* and add *ed* to verbs ending in *y*. married   _____

Future Tense Rule

1. Use the main verb with *will* or *shall*.   will sing   _____

Regular or Irregular?

Rule
8

Write the past tense of each verb below. Decide whether the verb is regular or irregular. Remember that irregular verbs do not follow the regular set of rules for changing tenses.

1. ride _____ **regular** **irregular**

2. hit _____ **regular** **irregular**

3. duck _____ **regular** **irregular**

4. spy _____ **regular** **irregular**

5. buy _____ **regular** **irregular**

6. run _____ **regular** **irregular**

7. stand _____ **regular** **irregular**

8. fan _____ **regular** **irregular**

9. cry _____ **regular** **irregular**

10. trade _____ **regular** **irregular**

11. look _____ **regular** **irregular**

12. tell _____ **regular** **irregular**

13. track _____ **regular** **irregular**

14. try _____ **regular** **irregular**

Name _____

Complete the Story

Complete the story by filling in each blank with the suggested verb in the tense requested.

Hank Aaron _____ a name you _____ in a list of baseball's Hall
　　　　　　　　(is—present)　　　　　　　　　　　　(find—future)

of Famers. Hank was _____ The Hammer because of his skill at batting. He
　　　　　　　　　　　　(nickname—past)

_____ down in history as the man who _____ Babe Ruth's home run record.
(go—future)　　　　　　　　　　　　　　　　　　　　(break—past)

He _____ 715 home runs in 1974. Many other records _____ on lists of his
　　(hit—past)　　　　　　　　　　　　　　　　　　　　　(appear—present)

baseball accomplishments. At the time of his retirement, he _____ records for most
　　　　　　　　　　　　　　　　　　　　　　　　　　　　(hold—past)

home runs, total bases, extra-base hits, runs batted in, and times at bat, among others.

Some of his records no longer _____, but Hank Aaron _____ remembered
　　　　　　　　　　　　　　(stand—present)　　　　　　　　(be—future)

as a great baseball player for as long as the game _____ played.
　　　　　　　　　　　　　　　　　　　　　　　(is—present)

Rule 9

There are several types of pronouns.

- **Subject pronouns** replace a noun used as the subject of the sentence.

I	you	he	she	it	we	they

They will arrive shortly.

She and he are cousins.

You and I were the first to finish the assignment.

- **Object pronouns** replace a noun used after an action verb or a preposition.

me	you	him	her	it	us	them

Please give the game to him when you have finished with it.

The principal picked her to lead the "Pledge of Allegiance."

Oscar tried to catch the leaves as they were falling all around us.

- **Reflexive pronouns** refer back to the subject.

myself	yourself	himself	herself	itself
ourselves	yourselves	themselves		

I looked at myself in the mirror.

Mary did this project all by herself.

The hikers found themselves far from camp.

Types of Pronouns

What Kind of Pronoun Is It?

Underline the pronouns in the sentences below. Write the type of pronoun (*subject, object,* or *reflexive*) on the line.

1. Carol does not want to complete the project by herself. _____

2. She will have more fun working with friends. _____

3. It will be easier to finish that way. _____

4. I like to read to my little brother. _____

5. Mom likes to watch us read together. _____

6. He likes stories about monsters. _____

7. Reading *Where the Wild Things Are* to him was fun. _____

8. We are going to Grandma's house for the weekend. _____

9. Grandma will probably bake cookies for us. _____

10. Hopefully, Grandpa won't eat all the cookies by himself. _____

11. My cousins Bill and Ted will take cookies for themselves. _____

Name _____

Pick the Proper Pronoun

Circle the correct pronoun or pronouns in each of the sentences.

1. Tim and (I   me) had a great time at Disneyland.

2. (We   Us) rode on long, winding roller coasters.

3. (They   Them) didn't scare (us   ourselves), though!

4. (He and I   Him and me) ate cotton candy and snowcones, too.

5. I bought (me   myself) a few souvenirs.

6. (We   Ourselves) both hope to visit Disneyland again some day.

7. Marty bought (myself   me) a new CD for my birthday.

8. (It   Itself) has my favorite songs on it.

9. (I   Me) got a card and money from (my   me) grandma.

10. Mom gave (I   me) a gift certificate to a restaurant.

11. (She and I   Her and me) will go out to dinner one night next week.

12. I like to go places just with (her   she).

Place the Pronouns

Complete the sentences by writing a pronoun from the box in each blank.

| us   we   themselves   them   they   he   their   her   I   his   ourselves   she |

1. Fifteen hikers found _____ lost in the woods.

2. _____ talked about the best way to find their way back to camp.

3. Kevin said _____ had an idea.

4. _____ idea was to break off into pairs and look for camp.

5. Pandora suggested, "We'll get _____ more lost that way!"

6. Kevin decided _____ was right.

7. Then all the hikers remembered words from _____ leader.

8. "_____ need to stay where we are and let our camp leader find us," Raymond declared.

9. "_____ have some trail mix to share while we wait," offered Tracy.

10. Linda said she would share _____ jerky.

11. "Read _____ stories from the book you brought, Raymond," suggested Kevin.

12. The hikers stayed put, and within an hour the camp leader had found _____.

There are more types of pronouns.

- **Indefinite pronouns** do not name the words they replace.

everyone	other	everything	each	anybody
nothing	somebody	something	no one	none

Anybody can see that the lamp is broken.

No one was home, so we left a note.

Somebody should pick up the dog's toys.

- **Demonstrative pronouns** point out a noun without naming it.

this	that	these	those

That is a terrific idea!

These are the best ones.

- **Interrogative pronouns** are used in asking a question.

who	whose	whom	which	what

What was that noise?

Who will be introducing the speaker?

With *whom* are you talking?

Which is your house?

Types of Pronouns

Indefinite Pronouns

Rule
10

Write an indefinite pronoun from the box below in each blank.

| everybody | both | anything | no one | few | everything | many | none | several |

_____ was excited about the trip to the rainforest. _____

in the class had ever been so far away from home. A _____ students were

nervous about flying in an airplane. _____ of us couldn't wait to get

on board.

Students could take _____ that would fit in one suitcase and a small

carry-on bag. _____ else had to be left at home. _____ of

the cases together could not weigh more than fifty pounds.

Identify Pronoun Types

Identify each of the words in bold as an *indefinite, demonstrative,* or *interrogative* pronoun. Write your response on the line.

1. "**What** was that noise?" Mom asked. _____

2. **No one** volunteered a response. _____

3. "Didn't **anybody** hear that crashing sound?" she asked again. _____

4. "**That** was a pretty loud noise," she continued. _____

5. "**Who** broke my flower vase?" she demanded, as she entered the study. _____

6. But **nobody** was even in the room except a guilty-looking cat! _____

7. **This** is the time of year for spring cleaning. _____

8. **Everyone** joins in the effort to spruce up the house and yard. _____

9. **Everything** starts looking better in no time. _____

10. **What** better time of year is there to make things look nice? _____

11. After all, **this** is the season when Grandma comes to visit! _____

Pronoun Detection

Underline the indefinite, demonstrative, and interrogative pronouns in the paragraph. Then write each of the underlined pronouns in the correct category below.

> Are you afraid of public speaking? When you have to give a speech, you may think, "What if my audience is bored?" or "Which opening statement will be the best to use?" Anyone can get nervous. Being prepared is the best way to calm yourself. Consider facial expressions, gestures, and visual aids. These can add to the effectiveness of your speech. Practice varying your vocal tones so everyone in your audience will stay awake. Think about your audience. Find ways to involve them in your presentation. Above all, don't panic! Prepare early and practice often, and you'll impress everyone in your audience.

Indefinite Pronouns	Demonstrative Pronouns	Interrogative Pronouns
_____	_____	_____
_____	_____	_____
_____	_____	_____

Rule 11

The antecedent of a pronoun is the noun or nouns to which the pronoun refers.

pronoun

After Marcus brushed his teeth, he went to bed.

antecedent

• The antecedent doesn't have to be in the same sentence as the pronoun.

pronoun

Phyllis was excited to get a new computer. It was a great gift.

antecedent

• A pronoun must agree with the antecedent in both gender and number.

Correct:	**Incorrect:**
Ramon has a new skateboard. **He** *took* **it** *to the skate park.*	*Ramon has a new skateboard.* **She** *took* **them** *to the skate park.*

Pronouns & Antecedents

Locate the Pronouns

A Circle the pronouns in these sentences. Draw a line from each pronoun to its antecedent.

1. Cathy and her friends are excited. They have never camped before.

2. Cathy's dad has been camping before. He will help them.

3. Cathy is packing a tent and a sleeping bag. She has put them in her car.

4. Cathy's dad will drive to the campground. Then he will help set up the tent.

5. After Cathy's friends pack, her dad will pick them up at their houses.

6. Cathy forgot her bug spray, but her dad picked it up.

7. Now, Cathy and her dad are ready to go. They have packed all they will need.

B Write a pronoun for each of these antecedents.

1. Cathy _____

2. Dad _____

3. Cathy and her friends _____

4. a tent _____

5. campers _____

6. Mom and I _____

7. Sister and me _____

8. hiking boots and socks _____

Pronoun Replacements

Rewrite each of the sentences. Replace the word or words in bold with a pronoun.

1. **Jonathan** has played the saxophone and the drums for three years.

_____

2. **Mrs. Kelsey** gives lessons to **Jonathan** on Monday afternoons.

_____

3. **Jonathan** is **Mrs. Kelsey's** best student.

_____

4. **Jonathan** listens to **Mrs. Kelsey** and plays **Jonathan's** instruments every day.

_____

5. **Jonathan** enjoys playing **the saxophone and the drums**.

_____

6. **Jonathan's** favorite instrument is the saxophone.

_____

7. **Jonathan** hopes to play **the saxophone** in a jazz band one day.

_____

Pronoun Agreement

Circle the correct pronouns in the paragraphs below.

Henry Barnard (1811–1900) was a busy man. (He She) was an educator, author, lawyer, and politician. (They He) served in the Connecticut legislature and as president of a number of colleges. In all of (his their) positions, (he she) worked to reform America's educational system. (They He) saw many ways to improve (them it).

First, (she he) pushed for the establishment of free high schools. (They He) were important, (it he) thought, because people of all classes should be educated. Then, (they he) organized the Bureau of Education. (Its Their) function was to conduct educational research. Additionally, (he they) wrote books and published journals on educational topics. (They It) were influential publications that helped shape the educational system in this country.

Rule 12

Possessive nouns need an apostrophe.
Possessive pronouns do not need an apostrophe.

- To make a **singular** noun show ownership, add an apostrophe (') and **s**.

the dog's bone
James's pet fish
the baseball player's cap

- To make the possessive of a **plural** noun that ends in **s**, add an apostrophe (').

the girls' clubhouse
the dancers' recital
the puppies' leashes

- To make the possessive of a **plural** noun that does not end in **s**, add an apostrophe (') and **s**.

the mice's holes
the geese's nests
the children's jackets

- When several people share a possession, add apostrophe (') **s** to the last noun.

Kelly, Henry, and Pete's class
Rudy and Moira's car

- **Possessive pronouns** do not require an apostrophe.

Used before a noun—my your his her our their

our school   my new kitten   his old truck

Stand alone—mine yours his hers its ours theirs

The notebook is mine.   Is that one yours?   No, it is hers.

Possessive Nouns & Pronouns

Who's the Owner?

Underline the possessive words in these sentences. Add apostrophes where they are needed to show ownership.

1. My family is going on a picnic in the park on Saturday.

2. Grandpa will carry Grandmas picnic basket full of food.

3. Moms tuna sandwiches will be placed in Dads cooler along with the drinks.

4. My brother is bringing his football.

5. Childrens games will include tag and water balloon wars.

6. Those who want to play the sport will bring baseball players equipment.

7. My nature-loving mother will look for bees hives and geeses nests.

8. Dad will likely read his book after lunch.

9. Uncle Todd and Aunt Darlas fishing poles will be used by all the kids.

10. Womens activities will include playing tennis and hiking on the trails.

11. Younger kids will play on the parks playground equipment.

12. The Wonderstads family picnic is always lots of fun.

Plural and Possessive Nouns

Circle the plural nouns in each sentence. Underline the possessive nouns. Add apostrophes where they are needed. One noun is both plural and possessive.

1. Zachs birthday piñata was filled with candies.

2. Karlas stick hit the piñata first.

3. Next, Johns stick hit the piñata.

4. The piñata finally broke with a hit from Zachs stick.

5. Birthday candies flew everywhere!

6. Zachs birthday guests picked up the candies.

7. Zachs neighbors came to join in the fun.

8. Even the dogs from down the street made their way to Zachs backyard.

9. The birthday guests, neighbors, and dogs all had a great time.

10. The afternoons game was a big hit.

11. Zach can't wait to go to all of his friends birthday parties next!

Name _____

Place Plurals and Possessives

Write the correct word in each sentence.

week's   weeks'

1. I spent one _____ worth of allowance at the movies last week.

2. It would cost three _____ worth of allowance to buy my favorite CD.

girls'   girl's

3. The _____ ball was lost after she hit it over the fence.

4. Three _____ bikes were parked outside Sally's house.

dollars'   dollars

5. Bring five _____ to the game Friday night for snacks.

6. My five _____ worth of penny candy lasted a long time!

lady's   ladies'

7. That _____ dress looks just like my mother's.

8. The Princeville _____ club took home the most awards from the fair.

feet   feet's

9. My _____ odor problem has finally gone away.

10. The school bus stops twenty _____ from my front door.

churches   church's

11. The _____ bell rings each Sunday morning at 9:00 a.m.

12. Five area _____ work together to collect food for the local food bank.

Rule 13

Adjectives describe nouns or pronouns.

- An **adjective** can tell what kind, which one, how many, or whose.

what kind   what kind

The mighty elephant pushed aside the large boulder.

what kind

Several migrating birds landed in the tree.

how many

which one   what kind

Those three girls created a colorful mural.

how many

The horses shook their manes.

whose

- **Demonstrative adjectives** point out a specific person, place, or thing.

This bike belongs to me.

I bought **that** coat last week.

These books are mine.

I don't like **those** shoes.

Adjectives

Locate the Adjectives

Circle all the adjectives in the paragraph.

In 1901, the determined Dr. Rupert Blue set out to kill every rat in San Francisco. The beautiful city had been struck with the deadly bubonic plague. Dr. Blue planned to destroy the frightening disease by killing the pesky rats that carried it. He decided to get rid of ugly dirt and garbage that served as the foul rats' homes and food sources. Many people in the large city helped him. Busy merchants cleaned their crowded stores. Concerned homemakers covered smelly household garbage in airtight metal cans. City workers poisoned sewer rats. School children scrubbed and mopped their classrooms. Butchers concreted the dirt floors of their meat plants. After seven years of work, city officials hosted an outdoor banquet to prove their city streets were now "clean enough to eat from." By 1909, about two million rats had been killed. The happy city was declared free of the horrible bubonic plague.

Name _____

Use Adjectives

Rule 13

A Complete these sentences by filling in the blanks with adjectives of your choice.

1. _____ _____ boats glide smoothly across the

_____ surface of the lake.

2. A _____ _____ tree sways in the breeze outside my

_____ window.

3. Karen's _____ and _____ father likes

_____ children and _____ animals.

4. The _____ racehorse often wins his races.

5. The _____ test worried the _____ children who did not study.

B Complete these sentences with the correct demonstrative adjectives.

| this | that | those | these |

1. _____ can opener works better than that one.

2. Do you know _____ people who waved to us?

3. Sara's office is in _____ building over there.

4. _____ shoes fit me the best of any I own.

Describe Nouns and Pronouns

Circle the adjectives in the sentences. Draw an arrow to the noun or pronoun each adjective tells about.

1. Jordan plays on the soccer team.

2. I like that flavor the best.

3. Kirby painted those beautiful landscapes.

4. Two full truckloads of sand were dumped under the swings in the playground.

5. My favorite soup is clam chowder topped with oyster crackers.

6. The football game will take place this Sunday.

7. Our friend has two tickets to the game.

8. My favorite aunt wore a long white veil at her wedding.

9. Kingston likes many fast and handsome cars.

10. Leah completed three pages of hard homework this morning.

11. Marlene practiced two difficult songs on the piano.

12. Altona, Indiana, is a small and friendly town.

Rule 14

Adjectives can make comparisons.

- **Comparative**—Most adjectives add **er** to compare two nouns. Some adjectives with two or more syllables use **more** or **less**.

  *An orca is **smaller** than a blue whale.*

  *The ballerina was **more graceful** than any other dancer.*

- **Superlative**—Most adjectives add **est** to compare three or more nouns. Some adjectives with two or more syllables use **most** or **least**.

  *Sarah is the **youngest** child in her family.*

  *She is the **least able** to do things for herself.*

Comparative & Superlative Adjectives

Find Comparisons

Circle the comparison adjectives in the following sentences. Decide whether each word or word phrase is a *comparative* or *superlative* adjective. Write your response on the line.

1. That was the most frightening lightning storm I have ever experienced! _____

2. Of the two, Kelly is the better flute player. _____

3. Nellie is the oldest child in her class. _____

4. Sam is the least likely to join the choir because he doesn't like to sing. _____

5. Ryan is shorter than Mike. _____

6. Tyler is less active than his athletic big brother. _____

7. I watched the most exciting movie ever last night! _____

8. Terri was happier than Timmy to be going to the zoo. _____

9. Sissy is the hardest worker in her group. _____

10. Watching a movie is more fun than reading a book. _____

Make Comparisons

Write the correct adjective in each sentence. Use the endings *er* or *est* and use *more* or *most* when they are needed. When you have finished, go back and write a **C** above every comparative adjective and an **S** above every superlative adjective.

1. Tina is the _____ piano player I know.
   (wonderful)

2. Tammy is a _____ runner than her friend Steve.
   (fast)

3. That is the _____ painting I've ever seen.
   (beautiful)

4. Riding a bike to school is _____ than walking there.
   (fun)

5. A swan's movements are _____ than those of a duck.
   (graceful)

6. Karen is the _____ student in her class.
   (young)

7. Leroy, the poodle, is the _____ of the Jacksons' two dogs.
   (small)

8. Ken is the _____ of the Carlton twins.
   (athletic)

9. The post office is _____ than the bank this afternoon.
   (busy)

10. The Cook-fast 2009 is the _____ of all the microwave models
    (expensive)

on display at Bob's Appliances on Sixth Street.

Use Comparisons

Use the comparative and superlative forms of the following adjectives in sentences of your own.

1. | pretty |

comparative _____

superlative _____

2. | loud |

comparative _____

superlative _____

3. | soft |

comparative _____

superlative _____

4. | careful |

comparative _____

superlative _____

5. | bad |

comparative _____

superlative _____

Rule 15

An adverb is a word that describes a verb, an adjective, or another adverb.

Adverbs can tell:

how: *We did our homework **carefully**.*
when: *They **often** play music together.*
where: *We went **away** to camp for a week.*
to what extent: *He **really** likes to play soccer.*

Adverbs can be used to make comparisons. They are changed in several ways:

- Add **er** or **est** to most short adverbs.

soon: *Come home **soon**.*
sooner: *The **sooner** they arrive, the sooner we can serve dinner.*
soonest: *Saturday is the **soonest** I can be there.*

hard: *Dad works **hard** to make the lawn look nice.*
harder: *Zippy, the puppy, plays **harder** than Rags, the old dog.*
hardest: *I study **hardest** just before a test.*

- Use **more** or **most** with most adverbs of two or more syllables and adverbs that end in **ly**.

| *carefully* | ***more** carefully* | ***most** carefully* |
| *often* | ***more** often* | ***most** often* |

- Some adverbs have special forms of comparison.

| *well* | *better* | *best* |
| *badly* | *worse* | *worst* |

Adverbs

Locate Adverbs

Underline the adverb in each sentence. Write *how*, *when*, *where*, or *to what extent* on the line to indicate what question each adverb answers.

1. Roger worked hard on his persuasive speech. _____

2. He researched late into the night. _____

3. He looked everywhere for information. _____

4. He wrote feverishly to complete his report on time. _____

5. On the day of the report, he arrived at school early. _____

6. When he was called on, Roger read his speech loudly. _____

7. He spoke clearly. _____

8. He used hand gestures frequently. _____

9. He wisely remembered to include audiovisual props. _____

10. He even engaged his audience often with interesting questions. _____

11. Roger thought he did a very good job overall. _____

12. Roger's teacher agreed that Roger presented an exceptionally _____
effective speech.

Make Adverb Comparisons

Write the correct adverb in each sentence. Use *more* or *most* when they are needed.

1. My mom drives _____ than my dad.
(carefully)

2. I scored _____ on my math paper than I did on my history report.
(well)

3. I did _____ in my health class than I did in science this semester.
(badly)

4. Tiasha works _____ than her friend Sissy.
(quickly)

5. That bird sings _____ than your other one.
(sweetly)

6. Keith asked _____ of all to be excused for lunch.
(politely)

7. Sally asked to get a drink _____ of all the kids in our class.
(often)

8. Mrs. Smith's class walked to the gym _____ than Mr. Dean's class.
(noisily)

What Is Described?

Rule
15

A On the lines provided, write whether each underlined adverb describes a *verb*, an *adjective*, or another *adverb*.

1. Kenny <u>really</u> likes to play baseball. _____

2. Susie exercises <u>daily</u>. _____

3. We will leave <u>very</u> early Saturday morning for the beach. _____

4. Mr. Kern writes a report about Tina's progress <u>daily</u>. _____

5. That was an <u>incredibly</u> beautiful sunset. _____

6. The bus driver drives to school <u>carefully</u> each day. _____

7. There was an <u>extremely</u> difficult word problem on last night's math homework. _____

8. Serge laughed <u>loudly</u> at the funny clowns in the parade. _____

9. Ask <u>politely</u> and you are more likely to get a good response. _____

10. Mavis worked <u>really</u> hard on her flute solo. _____

11. Clint <u>never</u> eats anything green. _____

B On the lines, write whether each underlined word is an *adjective* or an *adverb*. Remember that an adjective describes a noun. An adverb describes a verb, adjective, or adverb.

1. Sandra is a <u>fast</u> runner. _____

2. Larry runs <u>fast</u>. _____

3. The <u>early</u> bird catches the worm. _____

4. I will be at the meeting <u>early</u>. _____

Rule 16

Prepositions and prepositional phrases relate a noun or pronoun to another word in the sentence.

- A **preposition** is used to show the relationship of a noun or pronoun to another word in the sentence. Here are some common prepositions:

about	behind	during	inside	through
above	below	for	of	to
after	between	from	off	under
at	down	in	on	with

- A **prepositional phrase** is made up of a preposition, its object, and all the words in between. The object of the preposition is the noun or pronoun that follows the preposition.

preposition   object

The pirates buried their treasure under a tree.

prepositional phrase

preposition   object

I kicked the ball between the goalposts.

prepositional phrase

Prepositions

Name _____

Insert Prepositional Phrases

Complete the sentences below by writing a prepositional phrase from the box in each blank.

in the front	across the street	after school	under the bridge
of the tree	behind the counter	for breakfast	down the hill
at the park	from my big brother	of cake	during summer vacation

1. Kerry likes to play _____.

2. The man _____ sold me this ice-cream bar.

3. _____ on Fridays, Kayla goes to dance class.

4. The teacher's desk is _____ of the classroom.

5. I ate a piece _____ for dessert.

6. The river water rushed _____ after the first snowmelt.

7. My best friend lives just _____ from me.

8. I like to eat cereal _____.

9. I plan to go to Pennsylvania _____.

10. The limb _____ broke off in the ice storm.

11. My brother and I raced _____ on our sleds.

12. A letter arrived _____ today.

Use Prepositional Phrases

Rule 16

A Write a sentence using each of these prepositional phrases.

1. in the end

   _____

   _____

2. through the back gate

   _____

   _____

3. from you

   _____

   _____

4. into the end zone

   _____

   _____

5. to my grandmother's house

   _____

   _____

6. around the world

   _____

   _____

B Now go back and underline the preposition in each phrase. Write an **O** above the object of the preposition.

Name _____

Find the Prepositional Phrases

Underline the prepositional phrases in the paragraphs. Circle the object of each preposition.

Mendoza is an important city in western Argentina. It sits at the foot of the Andes Mountains. A highway and a railroad both cross the Andes from Mendoza into Chile. Much of the wine and fruit produced in Argentina comes from Mendoza. Mendoza is also home to two large universities.

Santiago is the capital city of Chile. It is also the cultural center of Chile. There are many universities, cathedrals, zoos, government buildings, and museums in the city. Tourism is important to Santiago's economy. Over the years, Santiago has survived the destructiveness of earthquakes, floods, and civil unrest. Today, it is a popular city to visit.

Honduras is home to the city of Puerto Cortés. Puerto Cortés lies in northwestern Honduras. It was established in 1525. Bananas and coffee are shipped around the world from this port city. The economy of Puerto Cortés relies on manufactured and traded goods.

Rule 17

A prepositional phrase can act as an adjective or an adverb.

- **Adjectival phrases** tell what kind or which one.

what kind

She lives in a house with a red door.

which one

The boy in the back seat was yelling loudly.

- **Adverbial phrases** tell how, when, or where.

Tell the story in your own words.

how

Mr. Kim jogs in the afternoon.

when

She ran behind the house.

where

Prepositional Phrases

Adjectival or Adverbial Phrase?

Rule 17

Underline the prepositional phrase in each sentence. Write *adjective* if it is an adjectival phrase or *adverb* if it is an adverbial phrase.

1. The winner of the contest won a big prize.   _____

2. After breakfast, the farmer feeds the cows.   _____

3. Paddle boats moved along the Missouri River.   _____

4. The frightened puppy hid under the back porch.   _____

5. The birthday candles with red stripes were flickering.   _____

6. The thirsty boy drank the juice in one swallow.   _____

7. All the ice in the lemonade began to melt.   _____

8. Jamal does his homework before dinner.   _____

9. Please handle the kittens with great care.   _____

10. Colorful flowers bloom in my garden.   _____

Add Adjectival Phrases

Rewrite the sentences by adding an adjectival phrase after each noun in bold. The first one has been completed for you as an example.

1. Our new **neighbors** will join us for dinner tonight.

Our new neighbors from Michigan will join us for dinner tonight.

2. The **boy** is my best friend.

_____

3. The **cornfield** is 35 acres wide.

_____

4. My grandmother lives in the **house**.

_____

5. Summer **temperatures** frequently reach 100 degrees.

_____

6. The **shade** provides some relief.

_____

7. The **cookie store** sells warm, delicious cookies.

_____

8. **Everyone** had a great time.

_____

Find Adverbial Phrases

Underline the adverbial phrase in each sentence. On the lines provided, indicate whether each phrase answers the question *how*, *when*, *where*, or *how long*.

1. Tim has math class in the morning. _____

2. Donna has dance lessons on Saturdays. _____

3. The cake baked for thirty-five minutes. _____

4. In the barn you will find the shovel. _____

5. The game was postponed for an hour. _____

6. She notified everyone by e-mail. _____

7. Grandpa and Grandma have been married for fifty years. _____

8. Sara rode her favorite horse in the pasture. _____

9. Spend about an hour a day practicing the piano. _____

10. After school, let's go ice-skating. _____

Rule 18

Words in a series, equal adjectives, and long dependent clauses need commas to separate them.

- to separate three or more words or phrases in a series.

    We ate pizza, chicken wings, and cake at his party.

    Sixteen students, two parents, and the teacher went on the field trip.

- to separate two or more adjectives that **equally** modify the same noun.*

Use a comma:

> *It's time to get rid of those smelly, old sneakers.*
>
> *She always asks interesting, intelligent questions.*

Don't use a comma:

> *Three big dogs are digging in the sand.*
>
> *Huge black clouds loomed over the mountains.*

- to separate a long dependent clause from the independent clause that follows it.

    Because it was so hot, we decided to stay indoors to play.

    long dependent clause   independent clause

    If you wish to know the answer, I will tell you.

    long dependent clause   independent clause

*See Notes to the Teacher on page 103 for additional information.

Comma Usage

Add Commas

Place commas properly in these sentences. Some sentences will require no commas.

1. Professional photographers take pictures of people landscapes historic landmarks and important events.

2. They may work for the media for a commercial firm or for themselves.

3. Photographers may work in the arts the sciences or the social sciences.

4. Ansel Adams took pictures of the rugged and wild American West.

5. Because he was a media photographer during the 1930s Walker Evans recorded scenes of the Great Depression.

6. Once a fashion photographer for *Vogue* magazine Cecil Beaton also worked as the official photographer of the British royal family.

7. Edwin Land invented the clever convenient Polaroid for his three-year-old daughter.

8. Edwin Land's daughter wondered why she couldn't see a photograph of herself as soon as her father took a picture of her.

9. Edwin Land worked hard and long to create the Polaroid.

10. If you like to take pictures you might consider becoming a professional photographer.

Add and Subtract Commas

Add or delete commas in the following sentences. Some sentences will require no corrections.

1. Elaine read a long intriguing novel last month.

2. It was the story of three boys, and their father.

3. Because the boys and their father went camping the story was set in the woods.

4. An angry bear, a violent thunderstorm, and a surprise visitor made the story a thriller.

5. Because she enjoyed the novel so much, Elaine recommended it to her friends.

6. Marcy Nancy and Taylor all enjoyed the story.

7. Kimberly likes to listen to soft, rock music.

8. She also likes country pop and hard rock tunes.

9. She likes the grand majestic sound of classical music as well.

10. While she does chores around the house Kimberly listens to music.

11. Listening to music somehow makes her work easier, and more fun.

Construct Sentences

Write sentences containing the words or phrases below in the order in which they appear. Add commas where they are needed.

1. five happy

_____

_____

2. After he finished washing the dishes

_____

_____

3. eager excited and determined

_____

_____

4. pretty little

_____

_____

5. drove to the store picked up the pizzas and returned to the house

_____

_____

6. While he waited in the lobby

_____

_____

7. balloons streamers and banners

_____

_____

A comma is used after introductory words and to set off the name of a person being spoken to.

- after **introductory words** such as **yes**, **no**, and **well** at the beginning of a sentence.

   Yes, that is Angela's little sister.

   No, you can't have dessert until you eat your broccoli.

   Well, I guess it's not too late to watch a movie.

- to set off the name of a person being spoken to.

   Austin, will you bring me that book?

   Come here, Steven, and pick up your report card.

   Did I see you at the game yesterday, Allen?

Comma Usage

Name _____

Introductory Commas

Add commas where they are needed in the dialogue.

Kevin I didn't expect to see you here. What a surprise!

Yes I'm meeting some of my friends from school for dinner.

Well do you come here often?

Yes as a matter of fact I do. I just love their desserts. You've got to try their blueberry pie Rhonda.

No I have my heart set on the chocolate chip cheesecake tonight.

Okay but next time you'll have to try the pie. It is absolutely awesome!

I promise you Kevin I'll try the blueberry pie next time I come.

You won't regret it Rhonda. Look there's Gordon!

Wow I haven't seen him in such a long time!

Hey is that Micah? I hope so because I'm ready to eat!

Well it was nice to see you Kevin. Have fun with your friends tonight.

Thanks! I will. See you later Rhonda.

Questions and Commas

Answer the following questions in complete sentences, using one of the introductory words given. Add commas where they are needed.

1. Is your birthday during the summer?

Yes _____

No _____

2. What do you consider to be your favorite food?

Well _____

3. How might you explain to a neighbor that you've hit a baseball through his window?

Sir _____

4. How might you ask your dad for a raise in your allowance?

Dad _____

5. Do you like apple pie?

Yes _____

No _____

6. What would you say if your friend asked you to go water-skiing?

Well _____

Okay _____

7. Do you know how to balance a checkbook?

Actually _____

Rephrase It

Restate the following sentences twice. In the first restatement, move the name to the middle of the sentence. In the second restatement, move the name to the end of the sentence. Remember to place commas where they are needed. The first one has been completed for you as an example.

1. Mom, please turn on the light.

Please, Mom, turn on the light.

Please turn on the light, Mom.

2. Grandma, may I help you bake a cake?

_____

_____

3. Thomas, I think your fever has finally broken.

_____

_____

4. Helen, I never knew that you attended Foothill Elementary School.

_____

_____

5. Daniel, please come in from the rain.

_____

_____

6. Stanley, imagine a world with no wars.

_____

_____

Rule 20

Commas and colons are used in specific instances.

Commas are used

• between the day of the month and the year.*

March 9, 2001   December 7, 1941

• between the name of a city and the state, province, or country.*

Denver, Colorado   Toronto, Ontario   Cairo, Egypt

• after the greeting and closing in a friendly letter.

Dear Alice,   Your friend,

Colons are used

• to separate the hour and minutes in time.   *9:15   12:00*

• after the greeting in a business letter.   *Dear Mrs. Jacobs:*

• before writing a list.   *Buy these at the store:*
                              cat food
                              kitty litter
                              flea collar

*See Notes to the Teacher on page 104 for additional information.

Commas & Colons

Punctuate a Friendly Letter

Add commas and colons where they are needed in this friendly letter.

1301 W. Quincy Street

Garrett Indiana

August 12 2009

Dear Grandma

　　Thanks for inviting my friends and me to your house next week. Mary Lisa and I expect to arrive around 600 on Sunday night. We will leave home around 600 on Saturday morning. Mary will drive from Denver Colorado to Omaha Nebraska. We'll find someplace to clean up eat dinner and sleep a few hours. We should be back on the road by 600 Sunday morning. Lisa will drive from Omaha to Garrett. Because we'll be arriving around suppertime we'll bring fast food from Charlie's Burgers in Garrett to share with you.

　　Last time we spoke you asked what we might like to do while vacationing in the Midwest. The following is a list of places we would like to visit

Auburn Cord Duesenberg Museum

Sandusky's sand dunes

Cedar Point Amusement Park

　　Although we would like to go to all the places on the list we really just want to spend time with you. Can't wait to see you!

Love

Doris

Punctuate a Schedule of Events

Rule
20

Add commas and colons where they are needed to this schedule of events.

Planned Events of the Ninth Annual

Young Writers' Conference

Dana College

Blair Nebraska

February 2 2009

830–930   Breakfast

930–1030   Keynote Speaker—Terry Willard from Seattle Washington

1030–1200 Choose one of the following writing sessions

          Developing Characters with Linda Algar from Ontario Canada

          Playful Poems with Thomas Timmer from Milwaukee Wisconsin

          Who Done It? with Sherry Hartley from Cove Oregon

          Setting the Scene with Jerry Brown from Pittsburgh Pennsylvania

1200–100   Lunch

100–230   Choose one of the following writing sessions

          Writing Nonfiction with Tyler Young from San Francisco California

          Newspaper Reporting with Duane Heffelfinger from Blair Nebraska

          Selling Script Ideas with Alfred Hurston from Los Angeles California

          Using Storyboards with Walter Disby from Riverton Wyoming

230–500   Critical Review Sessions

500–600   Dinner

600–1000   Viewing of Shakespearean play in Lincoln Nebraska

Name _____

Comma or Colon?

Fill in each blank below with a comma or a colon.

1. Isaac Asimov was born on January 2_ 1920.

2. Although he spent his adult years in America_ he was born in Petrovichi_ Russia.

3. Isaac Asimov was both a scientist and an author. A typical workday for the busy man might have looked like this_

9_00–12_00   Work on latest book

1_00–3_00   Teach science class at Boston University of Medicine

3_00–6_00   Conduct scientific research

4. Isaac Asimov's writings included the following_ science fiction_ humor_ history_ mysteries_ and classical translations.

5. Because he was able to entertain and inform_ his four hundred-plus books were immediately successful.

6. Isaac Asimov titles include the following_ *The Foundation Trilogy_ Foundation and Earth_* and *The Naked Sun.*

7. The prolific writer and esteemed scientist died on April 6_ 1992.

Use commas to set apart an appositive from the rest of the sentence.

An **appositive** is a word or phrase that renames the noun or pronoun before it.

appositive

<u>Mrs. Burton</u>, *a high school teacher , was at the ceremony.*
noun

appositive

<u>Carter</u>, *a math whiz , won an award.*
noun

appositive

<u>Our principal</u>, *Mr. Grant , presented the awards.*
noun

Comma Usage

Set Apart Appositives

Set apart the appositives in these sentences by adding commas where they are needed.

1. Mary Dyer a Quaker was killed in 1660 for living in Boston a city that once prohibited Quaker residency.

2. The 1931 Nobel Peace Prize winner Jane Addams founded Hull House a social service settlement in Chicago.

3. Dorothy Day an author established "hospitality houses" for Great Depression victims during the 1930s.

4. *Aesop's Fables* animal-based stories with morals are the most widely read fables in the world.

5. A book of the teachings of Confucius *Lun Yü* has influenced both Eastern and Western thinkers.

6. The Hippocratic Oath an oath written by the Greek physician Hippocrates continues to be used in the medical field today.

7. Andorra a country located in southwestern Europe covers 181 square miles.

8. A group of ten islands southwest of Africa the Cape Verde Islands are volcanic in origin.

9. Kiribati formally the Gilbert Islands is comprised of 33 islands in the west-central Pacific Ocean.

10. Mauritania rich in iron ore and poor in plants and animals is located in the Sahara Desert.

Name _____

Locate Appositives

Circle the appositives in the paragraphs below.

Dekalb High School, my sister's school, celebrated graduation last Saturday. My sister was not in the graduating class, but her friend, Tamara White, was. My sister and I attended the ceremony. Mr. Dean, the president of a local college, gave a speech, "Life on the Outside." It was a humorous look at being a young adult.

Following Mr. Dean's speech, awards were presented. The school's computer whiz, Martin Elliott, won an academic award. Linda Baker, student body president, won a spirit award. The winner of the community service award was my sister's friend, Tamara, who set up programs at the school for recycling, visiting the elderly, and beautifying the campus.

Finally, Mr. Kraft, the principal, presented diplomas. Because Tamara's last name, White, is at the end of the alphabet, she received her diploma last. Then the graduates tossed their hats, and my sister and I clapped loudly for Tamara, a good friend of my sister.

Write with Appositives

Rule 21

The sentences below all contain spaces for appositives and other information. Fill in the spaces based on facts from your own life. The first one has been completed for you as an example.

1. My mom, <u>Doris Cooksey</u>, lives in Colorado.

2. My favorite movie, _____, stars _____.

3. My favorite holiday, _____, occurs in the month of _____.

4. My favorite pet, a _____, is named _____.

5. My favorite television show, _____, is broadcast at

_____ o'clock.

6. One of my best friends, _____, is really good at _____.

7. An author whom I enjoy, _____, wrote a book entitled

_____.

8. _____, a book by _____, is one of my favorites.

9. My favorite type of music, _____, is also loved by _____.

10. My teacher, _____, has _____ eyes.

A direct quotation has specific rules of punctuation and capitalization.

- **Quotation marks** are placed before and after a speaker's exact words.

  "What a wonderful surprise!" exclaimed Mr. Chang.

  "Did you make that mess in the kitchen?" asked Dwight's mother.

- Capitalize the first word of each sentence in a quotation.

  *Roberto chanted, "**W**e won the game! **W**e won the game!"*

  *"**Y**ou boys should be very proud of yourselves," the coach remarked. "**Y**ou have practiced very hard."*

- We usually use a comma to separate the quotation from the rest of the sentence.

  "This is a good book," stated Tony.

  Tony stated, "This is a good book."

Quotation Marks

Add Quotation Marks

Add quotation marks to these sentences. Underline the speaker.

1. Tom asked, Did you write this story, Jim?

2. Yes, Jim replied. It was an assignment for English class.

3. It is a very good story, Jim, Tom said. Do you mind if I share it with my friends?

4. While smiling shyly, Jim stammered, That would be fine, Tom.

5. Would you like to come to my birthday party, Shelly? asked Katie.

6. That would be fun, Shelly responded. What would you like as a gift?

7. I like arts and crafts supplies, Katie replied.

8. Then I know just the gift for you! Shelly exclaimed.

9. Where have you been? complained Jacob. We have all been waiting for you!

10. I had to take care of my little brother, Tyler explained.

11. Oh, I forgot about that! Nelson said. I was supposed to tell you that before, Jacob. I'm sorry I forgot to relay your message, Tyler.

12. That's okay, said Tyler. I'm here now, so let's start the movie.

Correct Quotations

Rewrite each sentence, adding quotation marks around each person's exact words.
Use capital letters and other punctuation marks where they are needed.

1. mom when does the dinner party start asked larry

_____

2. that was the best movie i've ever seen exclaimed marcus.

_____

3. before the big test, my teacher reminded us erase your first choice completely if you decide
to change your answer.

_____

4. marty said she would be here by three o'clock cecil reported.

_____

5. royal said i like to play volleyball

_____

6. the whole team chanted we are the champions we are the champions

_____

7. have you ever been to this restaurant before tiasha cindy asked

_____

8. you will get a good grade on today's test i told myself.

_____

To Quote or Not to Quote?

Rule 22

Some of the following sentences contain direct quotes. Some of them do not. Add capital letters, commas, and quotation marks only where they are necessary. Some sentences will require no changes.

1. Mr. Fires said that he should have our car fixed by Friday afternoon.

2. Mrs. Fields reminded me you don't have to get a perfect score; you just have to do your best.

3. Candy explained I was named after my aunt, not after a food!

4. Tony asked if I could help him with his homework.

5. Fred told me never to touch an electrical appliance with wet hands.

6. Samatha told me that my grandmother will be in town next week.

7. This is an excellent CD Anthony proclaimed.

8. Uncle Jack told me that he would be in town next week.

9. Mom told me don't tell Dad what we got him for Christmas.

10. Nancy said she was planning to attend the Petersons' housewarming party.

Titles of books, movies, plays, magazines, songs, stories, etc., are treated in specific ways.

- Capitalize the first word, the last word, and every word in between except for articles *(the, a, an)*, short prepositions, and short conjunctions.

Night of the **T**wisters

In the **Y**ear of the **B**oar and **J**ackie **R**obinson

A **P**izza the **S**ize of the **S**un

- When you write in handwriting, underline the titles of books, movies, plays, and television programs, and the names of newspapers and magazines.

<u>The Lost World</u> (movie)

<u>Smoky Night</u> (book)

<u>National Geographic</u> (magazine)

- If you are using a word processor, use italics instead of underlining.

The Lost World (movie)

Smoky Night (book)

National Geographic (magazine)

- Use quotation marks around the titles of stories, magazine articles, essays, songs, and most poems.

"America" (song)

"Kayaking in Canada" (article)

"The Highwayman" (poem)

Titles

Punctuate Titles

Rewrite these sentences using the correct punctuation for each title.

1. The book entitled Three by Finney by Jack Finney includes the stories The Woodrow Wilson Dime, Marion's Wall, and The Night People.

_____

_____

2. Moonlight Bay, a song written in 1912, was written by Edward Madden and Percy Wenrich.

_____

_____

3. This month's edition of Stellar Students magazine contains an excellent article entitled Test-Taking Tricks.

_____

_____

4. My local newspaper is called The Fairfield Press.

_____

_____

5. The Shel Silverstein book Where the Sidewalk Ends contains a poem entitled Where the Sidewalk Ends.

_____

_____

6. Last weekend, I attended a play called Johnny Came Marching Home.

_____

_____

Capital Letters in Titles

Rewrite the sentences using the correct capitalization.

1. Rita watched the movie <u>honey, i shrunk the kids</u> for the fourth time last night.

_____

_____

2. My class sang "by the light of the silvery moon" for Grandparents' Day.

_____

_____

3. "nicki's new neighbor" is my favorite story in our literature book, <u>stories from around the world</u> <u>and right next door.</u>

_____

_____

4. Sarah's essay, "why we have to learn math," was well researched.

_____

_____

5. During career day, a reporter from <u>the market valley press</u> shared his latest story, "teens and teaching," with our class.

_____

_____

6. I wrote a poem entitled "mine," which will be included in our school's literary journal, <u>panther pride.</u>

_____

_____

Write Titles

Complete these sentences by writing titles. Be sure to underline titles of books, magazines, newspapers, movies, and television programs. Use quotation marks for stories, magazine articles, essays, songs, and poems.

1. If I wrote a poem about sunlight, I would call it _____.

2. _____ would be a great name for a song about traveling.

3. One of my favorite movies is entitled _____.

4. A magazine article about training horses might be entitled _____.

5. A magazine dedicated to medical issues might be entitled _____.

6. _____ is the name of a newspaper available to people who live in my community.

7. I once wrote a story in school called _____.

8. Someone I know loves to watch the television program _____.

9. An essay on the importance of cooperation might be called _____.

10. One of my favorite books is entitled _____.

Rule 24

Negative words and the pronouns **I**, **me**, **they**, and **them** follow specific usage rules.

A **negative** is a word that means *no* or *not*. Use only one negative in a sentence.

Correct:	**Incorrect:**
I **didn't** bring any lunch today. I have **no** lunch today.	I **didn't** bring **no** lunch today.

Use **I** and **they** in the subject.

> **I** need to be home by six o'clock.
> **They** won't be able to come to the game.

Use **me** and **them** in the predicate or after a preposition.

> Will you help **me** bake some cookies?
> George took a trip to Marine World with **them**.

Name yourself last.

> Morris and **I** like to build unusual kites.
> Would you like to go to the park with Sam and **me**?

Word Usage

Find the Errors

A There is an error in each of the sentences below. Rewrite each sentence correctly.

1. I didn't bring no lunch money to school today.

   _____

2. I and my brother like to play football together.

   _____

3. Me and Anthony are best friends.

   _____

4. Them don't think they can make it to class today.

   _____

5. They've been waiting longer, so serve they first.

   _____

6. The postmaster gave the package to Mom and I.

   _____

B Decide whether each sentence below contains an error. Write *correct* or *incorrect* on the line.

1. Marty and me are going to the concert Saturday night.   _____

2. Stella likes to go to the store with him and me.   _____

3. Krista has given them a gift certificate.   _____

4. She don't like no mushrooms in her salad.   _____

5. Would you like to bake cookies with me and Grandma?   _____

Pick the Proper Word

Circle the correct word in each sentence below.

1. Ted and (me   I) are in the same class this year.

2. I want to go with (they   them) to the ice-skating rink.

3. Their grandfather lives with (they   them).

4. I (ain't   am not) going to the track meet.

5. I don't have (any   no) extra pencils in my backpack today.

6. Dad is meeting Mom and (I   me) at the airport.

7. (They   Them) are excellent neighbors.

8. I don't want (no   any) dressing on my salad.

9. When my pizza comes with olives, I pick (they   them) off.

10. Randolph, Ryder, and (I   me) are working on a project together.

11. (Them   They) are very artistic.

12. I haven't gotten (no   any) letters from (they   them) all month.

Write It Right

Using the following words correctly, write sentences of your own.

1. I _____

2. they _____

3. me _____

4. them _____

5. didn't _____

6. don't _____

7. no _____

8. not _____

9. never _____

10. none _____

11. nothing _____

12. won't _____

Rule 25

Some words are easily confused.
Take care to use **can/may**, **sit/set**, **lie/lay**, **good/well**, and **who's/whose** correctly.*

• can—may

Use *can* to tell that someone is able to do something.

*Norman **can** hit the ball really far.*

Use *may* to ask or give permission to do something.

***May** I have another piece of pie?*

• sit—set

Use *sit* to mean "stay seated."

*Please **sit** in the green chair.*

Use *set* to mean "to put or place."

*She **set** her homework on the desk.*

• lie—lay

Use *lie* to mean "to rest or recline."

*I like to **lie** in the shade of the tree.*

Use *lay* to mean "to put or place."

*Did you **lay** the box on the bench?*

• good—well

Good is an adjective. Use *good* to describe nouns.

*Mom looks **good** in her new dress.*

Well is an adverb. Use *well* to describe verbs.

*It fits her **well**.*

• who's—whose

Use *who's* to mean "who is."

***Who's** banging on the front door?*

Use *whose* to show ownership.

***Whose** backpack is that?*

*See Notes to the Teacher on page 104 for additional information.

Word Usage

Catch the Errors

Decide which sentences have errors. Cross them out and rewrite them correctly on the lines below.

1. Audrey can sing like an angel.

2. Can I have an ice-cream cone?

3. You may sharpen your pencil before the bell rings.

4. Please set down at your desk and begin your work.

5. If Randy sets on top of that counter, he will break it.

6. Set your books under your desk until the test is over.

7. Good posture requires you to sit up straight.

8. If you are not feeling well, you should lie down.

9. Lay your backpack on the table so you will remember to take it to school.

10. Sally is a good soccer player.

11. Ted also plays pretty good.

12. Whose your teacher this year?

13. Who's going to be at the lake this summer?

14. Who's cat keeps coming to our front door?

_____

_____

_____

_____

_____

Complete the Sentences

Complete each sentence by filling in the blank with a word from the box.

can	may	sit	set	lie	lay	good	well	who's	whose

1. Mom, _____ I go to the park with Ricky?

2. _____ your tools on the workbench when you finish the job.

3. Teresa plays the piano _____.

4. _____ house is on the corner by the mall?

5. My brother _____ eat more pizza in one sitting than anyone I know.

6. Never _____ in the sun without wearing sunscreen.

7. _____ that new boy in Mr. Baker's class?

8. I will _____ in the back row if there are no other seats available.

9. That's a _____ pizza your mom baked.

10. You can _____ your books on the table by the door.

Which One Works?

Circle the correct word in each sentence.

1. That's Daniel, (whose   who's) my brother's friend.

2. The play we attended at school was (good   well).

3. We always (sit   set) the video that needs to go back to the store by the front door.

4. I (can   may) do twenty-five push-ups.

5. The teacher said we (can   may) use a calculator to do problems 20 through 25.

6. I will (lie   lay) your notebook on your desk after I copy the notes I missed yesterday.

7. Nellie speaks (good   well), but she is uncomfortable in front of large crowds.

8. You can (lie   lay) down for a quick nap before dinner if you are tired from the drive.

9. (Who's   Whose) car is that parked beside your fence?

10. My five-month-old brother already (sits   sets) up by himself.

Grammar and Punctuation Review
Part A, Rules 1–12
Fill in the bubble next to the correct answer.

A1. Which of these is an exclamatory sentence?
Ⓐ Take your jacket to the game.
Ⓑ Which road should I take?
Ⓒ Stop shouting!

A2. In which sentence is the simple subject underlined?
Ⓐ The morning <u>sun</u> lit up the sky.
Ⓑ <u>The new student</u> sat quietly at her desk.
Ⓒ He chopped <u>firewood</u> for his neighbors.

A3. In which sentence is the complete predicate underlined?
Ⓐ All of my friends <u>know how to ski</u>.
Ⓑ <u>Autumn leaves</u> crunched under his feet.
Ⓒ The careful mountain climber <u>reached</u> the summit.

A4. Which of these is a compound sentence?
Ⓐ Nate and Mia have a new kitten.
Ⓑ The kitten has black fur, but his feet are white.
Ⓒ They feed the kitten in the morning and in the afternoon.

A5. Which of these should be capitalized?
Ⓐ volunteer   Ⓑ democracy   Ⓒ united nations

A6. Which of these is the plural form of the noun **thief**?
Ⓐ thiefs   Ⓑ thiefes   Ⓒ thieves

A7. Which kind of verb is underlined?
Which painting <u>is</u> yours?
Ⓐ action verb   Ⓑ linking verb   Ⓒ helping verb

A8. In which sentence does the subject agree with the verb?
Ⓐ The referee call a foul.
Ⓑ The night sky was filled with stars.
Ⓒ All of the student work together.

Grammar and Punctuation Review

Part A, Rules 1–12 (continued)

Fill in the bubble next to the correct answer.

A9. Which verb tense is used in this sentence?
The band will march in the parade.
- Ⓐ past tense
- Ⓑ future tense
- Ⓒ present tense

A10. Which of these is the present tense of the verb **apply**?
- Ⓐ applies
- Ⓑ applyes
- Ⓒ applys

A11. Which of these is a past tense verb?
- Ⓐ eat
- Ⓑ knew
- Ⓒ think

A12. Which of these is a subject pronoun?
- Ⓐ we
- Ⓑ her
- Ⓒ them

A13. Which of these is a reflexive pronoun?
- Ⓐ him
- Ⓑ they
- Ⓒ myself

A14. Which of these is an interrogative pronoun?
- Ⓐ who
- Ⓑ these
- Ⓒ somebody

A15. What is the antecedent of the underlined word?
Joaquim wrote a poem. <u>It</u> was about a lake.
- Ⓐ Joaquim
- Ⓑ poem
- Ⓒ lake

A16. Which of these is a possessive pronoun?
- Ⓐ yours
- Ⓑ men's
- Ⓒ Karla's

Grammar and Punctuation Review

Part B, Rules 13–25

Fill in the bubble next to the correct answer.

Which words are adjectives?

B1. Ⓐ those   Ⓑ annoy   Ⓒ chemist

B2. Ⓐ lather   Ⓑ career   Ⓒ thinner

B3. Which word is an adverb?
Ⓐ rely
Ⓑ pulley
Ⓒ generally

B4. Which word or words should go in the blank?
Hiroko rides her bike _____ than Judy.
Ⓐ carefully
Ⓑ more carefully
Ⓒ most carefully

B5. Which of these is a prepositional phrase?
Ⓐ a glorious day
Ⓑ through the garden gate
Ⓒ poisonous snakes

B6. What does the underlined prepositional phrase tell?
The rabbit hopped <u>away from the tree</u>.
Ⓐ where   Ⓑ when   Ⓒ how

Which of these uses commas correctly?

B7. Ⓐ A bright, shining moon rose over the hill.
Ⓑ A bright, shining, moon rose over the hill.
Ⓒ A bright, shining, moon, rose over the hill.

B8. Ⓐ Because Kenny was late he missed the bus.
Ⓑ Because Kenny was late, he missed the bus.
Ⓒ Because, Kenny was late, he missed the bus.

Grammar and Punctuation Review
Part B, Rules 13–25 (continued)
Fill in the bubble next to the correct answer.

Which of these uses commas correctly?

B9.
Ⓐ Well I never would have thought of that Tom.
Ⓑ Well, I never would have thought of that Tom.
Ⓒ Well, I never would have thought of that, Tom.

B10.
Ⓐ They moved into a new house on March 23, 1999.
Ⓑ Their new street address is 2368, Sunset Drive.
Ⓒ Their new home is in Sierra, Vista Arizona.

B11.
Ⓐ My best friend Celia, lives next door.
Ⓑ My best friend, Celia lives next door.
Ⓒ My best friend, Celia, lives next door.

Which of these is correct?

B12.
Ⓐ Scott asked, "Have you seen my backpack?"
Ⓑ Scott asked "Have you seen my backpack?"
Ⓒ Scott asked, "have you seen my backpack?"

B13.
Ⓐ "People" is Cory's favorite magazine.
Ⓑ "Moon River" is Allison's favorite song.
Ⓒ "Good Night Moon" is my sister's favorite book.

B14.
Ⓐ They didn't ask I any questions.
Ⓑ They didn't ask me no questions.
Ⓒ They didn't ask me any questions.

B15.
Ⓐ Can I sit on the couch?
Ⓑ May I sit on the couch?
Ⓒ May I set on the couch?

B16.
Ⓐ Who's dog is setting in my favorite chair?
Ⓑ Whose dog is sitting in my favorite chair?
Ⓒ Whose dog is setting in my favorite chair?

Name

Rule	Skill	Activity Pages Circle when completed			Review Questions		
					Number	Correct	Not Correct
1	Identify four kinds of sentences.	4	5	6	A1		
2	Identify simple & complete subjects and predicates.	8	9	10	A2/A3		
3	Identify compound sentences.	12	13	14	A4		
4	Identify common, proper, singular, and plural nouns.	16	17	18	A5		
5	Form plural nouns.	20	21	22	A6		
6	Identify action, linking, and helping verbs. Use correct subject-verb agreement.	24	25	26	A7/A8		
7	Identify present, past, and future tense verbs.	28	29	30	A9		
8	Form present, past, and future tense verbs.	32	33	34	A10/A11		
9	Identify subject, object, and reflexive pronouns.	36	37	38	A12/A13		
10	Identify indefinite, demonstrative, and interrogative pronouns.	40	41	42	A14		
11	Identify the antecedent of a pronoun.	44	45	46	A15		
12	Form possessive nouns and pronouns.	48	49	50	A16		
13	Identify adjectives.	52	53	54	B1		
14	Use comparative and superlative adjectives.	56	57	58	B2		
15	Identify adverbs. Use adverbs to make comparisons.	60	61	62	B3/B4		
16	Identify prepositions and prepositional phrases.	64	65	66	B5		
17	Identify adjective and adverbial phrases.	68	69	70	B6		
18	Use commas to separate words in a series, adjectives that equally modify the same noun, and dependent clauses from independent clauses.	72	73	74	B7/B8		
19	Use commas after introductory words and to set off the names of people being spoken to.	76	77	78	B9		
20	Use commas in dates, addresses, and letters. Use colons with time, in letters, and with lists.	80	81	82	B10		
21	Use commas to set apart an appositive from the rest of the sentence.	84	85	86	B11		
22	Use quotation marks.	88	89	90	B12		
23	Write titles.	92	93	94	B13		
24	Use negatives. Use the words *I/they, me/them*.	96	97	98	B14		
25	Use the words *can/may, sit/set, lie/lay, good/well*, and *who's/whose*.	100	101	102	B15/B16		

Notes to the Teacher

Rule 3, page 11

The rule states that compound sentences are **usually** joined by conjunctions. A semicolon may also replace a comma and conjunction in a compound sentence.

Simple sentences: *He broke the window.*
It was an accident.

Compound sentence: *He broke the window; it was an accident.*

Rule 8, page 31

The present tense endings *s* and *es* are used only with third person singular nouns and pronouns (*he, she, it, Grandma, Mr. Jones,* etc.). The distinction between first person and third person may need to be explained to nonnative speakers.

Rule 18, page 71

1. Note that the use of a comma to separate the two independent clauses of a compound sentence is addressed in Rule 3.

2. Here are two tests to use to determine if adjectives are modifying a noun equally:

   • Put *and* between the adjectives. If the sentence sounds correct, use a comma.

   > *It's time to get rid of those smelly, old sneakers.*
   > *It's time to get rid of those smelly **and** old sneakers.*
   > (*and* sounds OK, so use a comma)

   > *Three big dogs are digging in the sand.*
   > *Three **and** big dogs are digging in the sand.*
   > (*and* sounds odd, so do not use a comma)

   • Switch the order of the adjectives. If the sentence sounds correct, the adjectives modify equally.

   > *It's time to get rid of those smelly, old sneakers.*
   > *It's time to get rid of those old, smelly sneakers.*
   > (sounds OK; use a comma)

   > *Three big dogs are digging in the sand.*
   > *Big three dogs are digging in the sand.*
   > (sounds odd; do not use a comma)

Notes to the Teacher

In running text, a comma follows as well as precedes both the year and the state, province, or country.

The events of April 18, 1775, have long been celebrated in song and story.
The electrical storms in Flagstaff, Arizona, are no less than spectacular.

Well is often confused with *good*.

- *Good* is an adjective, and *well* is **usually** an adverb.

   *She is a **good** musician.*
   *She plays both the piano and the guitar **well**.*

   *I received a **good** grade on the social studies test.*
   *All the time spent studying served me **well**.*

- Both *well* and *good* are correct in this instance.

   *"After all that food, I don't feel **well**," groaned Melvin.*
   *"I don't feel **good**, either," complained Marvin.*

- Although both *well* and *good* are correct here, the meaning in sentence two may be unclear.

   *You don't look **well**. (You look sick.)*
   *You don't look **good**. (It could be that you look sick,
   or it could be that your appearance isn't appealing.)*

Answer Key

Page 4

1. ! exclamatory OR . declarative
2. . declarative
3. ? interrogative
4. . declarative OR ! exclamatory
5. . imperative
6. . declarative
7. . imperative
8. . declarative
9. ? interrogative
10. ! exclamatory OR . imperative

Page 5

1. ? interrogative
2. ! exclamatory OR . declarative
3. . imperative
4. . declarative
5. . declarative
6. . declarative
7. . declarative
8. . imperative
9. ? interrogative

Page 6

Answers will vary, but sentences should exemplify the stated sentence types.

Page 8

1. My best (friend) lives in Thailand.
2. Her (name) is Roongthip.
3. Roongthip's (name) means "Rainbow" in Thai.
4. Roongthip's (culture) is different from mine.
5. Thai (money) looks different from United States money.
6. The Thai (language) uses a different alphabet.
7. Thai (foods) use different spices from those I am used to.
8. Thai (cities) are filled with intricate architecture.
9. Roongthip's (world) is different from mine.
10. My (friend) and (I) love learning about each other's cultures.

Page 9

1. My school (offers) many extra clubs and classes.
2. My brother (plays) chess with the chess club.
3. My friend Sam (plays) baseball.
4. I (sing) with the school choir.
5. Members of the Community Service Club (visit) elderly people who live alone.
6. They also (pick) up litter around our town.
7. Members of the journalism class (write) our school newspaper.
8. The school marching band (marches) in parades.
9. The pep band (plays) at football games.
10. Everyone (participates) in something special at our school.

Page 10

Answers will vary for phrases that are not complete sentences because students must add words of their own to create complete sentences.

1. Not a complete sentence
2. Karen is going to Disneyland this summer.
3. I love strawberries.
4. Not a complete sentence
5. Not a complete sentence
6. Not a complete sentence
7. Not a complete sentence
8. Not a complete sentence
9. He's lost!
10. It's basketball season.

Page 12

1. Movies are exciting, (but) books are better.
2. I like summer vacation, (yet) I am always glad when school starts again.
3. We enjoy the beautiful sights in San Francisco, (so) we chose to vacation in that city.

Page 12 (continued)

4. I went to the bank, (and) then I did my shopping.
5. Art museums are fun to visit, (but) you need to be prepared to spend the day in them.
6. Beautiful flowers blossom, (and) then they fade away.
7. Race dogs are fast, (but) racehorses are faster.
8. English class is hard for me, (but) math class is easy.
9. Frightening tornadoes destroy property, (and) earthquakes are devastating, too.
10. Martha and Jerry will go to the beach today, (or) they will watch a movie.

Page 13

1. I love hamburgers, but I hate hot dogs.
2. I may go to Mexico this summer, or I may go to France.
3. After school I'm going shopping, and I'm going to buy a new backpack.
4. Christmas is my favorite holiday, but I also enjoy Thanksgiving.
5. Your birthday is on Monday, but we'll celebrate this Sunday afternoon.
6. The Little Mermaid is a great book, but The Frog Prince is even better.

Page 14

1. simple
2. simple
3. compound
4. compound
5. compound
6. compound
7. simple
8. simple
9. compound

Page 16

1. common, plural
2. proper, singular
3. common, plural
4. proper, singular
5. proper, singular
6. common, plural
7. proper, singular
8. common, singular
9. common, plural
10. proper, singular
11. common, plural
12. proper, singular

Page 17

1. Doris Cooksey, American Family Insurance Company
2. Denver, Colorado
3. Bailey, Colorado
4. Doris, Honda Accord
5. Dennis, Francisco, Ramona
6. Peterson Street
7. Doris, Burger Hut
8. Francisco, Dennis, Mega Burger
9. Doris, Ramona
10. Doris, Denver, Bailey

Page 18

1. Tobias, Nolan, oldies
2. Nolan's, group, Beach Boys
3. Tobias, Simon and Garfunkel
4. boys, movies
5. Nolan's, actor, James Stewart
6. Tobias, Joan Crawford, movies
7. Nolan, Tobias, ghost towns
8. games, Old Maid, Go Fish
9. boys', books, classics, <u>The Adventures of Tom Sawyer</u>
10. Tobias, Nolan, historians

Page 20

stores, gifts, boxes, carts, shelves, benches, ladies, babies, blocks, presents, goodies

Page 21

1. deer
2. moose
3. people
4. cactuses OR cacti
5. hypotheses
6. crises
7. women
8. men
9. sheep
10. axes
11. series
12. feet

Page 21 (continued)

Answers will vary, but all plural forms that follow the stated rules should be identified as *regular*, and those that don't should be called *irregular*.

Page 22

Sentences will vary, but should include the following plurals:

1. parties, cakes
2. cows, calves
3. wishes, beliefs
4. strawberries, patches
5. series, games
6. rules, policies
7. dentists, teeth
8. ducks, geese
9. men, women
10. feet, children

Page 24

1. Mrs. Baker <u>is</u> forty-two years old.
2. She works at an automobile manufacturing plant in Michigan.
3. She has been working there for twenty years.
4. In twenty more years, she will retire.
5. Mr. Baker <u>was</u> forty-two years old last year.
6. He <u>is</u> a year older than Mrs. Baker.
7. He <u>is</u> a librarian at a school library.
8. He finds books for students.
9. He has been helping students for fifteen years.
10. He likes his job.
11. He will work in the library for twenty more years.
12. Then he and Mrs. Baker will travel around the country.

Page 25

1. linking, action
2. action, linking
3. action, linking
4. action, linking
5. linking, action
6. linking, action

Page 26

1. has
2. gets
3. enjoy
4. brings
5. bake
6. gives
7. lets
8. are
9. take
10. plays
11. like
12. play
13. throw
14. finds
15. wants

Page 28

1. lived—past
2. was—past
3. is remembered—present
4. are loved—present
5. are—present
6. will continue—future
7. is, writes—present
8. are known—present
9. was written—past
10. was, came out—past
11. is—present
12. will call—future

Page 29

1. worked
2. hopes
3. has
4. hopes
5. built
6. has
7. will
8. will spend
9. is
10. moved
11. has
12. hopes

Page 30

Some students may also identify infinitives such as *to play, to judge,* etc.

> **PR**
> Thomas <u>loves</u> to play the piano. He
> **P**
> <u>took</u> his first lesson at the age of five.
> **PR**
> He <u>practices</u> for an hour each day. He
> **PR**
> especially <u>likes</u> to play classical music.
> **P**
> He first <u>heard</u> classical music when
> **P**
> he <u>began</u> his lessons. At a concert
> **F**
> tomorrow night, he <u>will play</u> his favorite
> piece, Mozart's "Allegro." The audience
> **F**
> <u>will enjoy</u> the concert because Thomas
> **PR**
> <u>is</u> an excellent pianist.

> **PR**
> Stacy <u>is</u> in her town's parade every
> **P**
> July. Last year she <u>marched</u> with her
> **PR**
> school band. This year she <u>is riding</u> her
> **F**
> horse. Next year she <u>will find</u> something
> **PR**
> else to do because she <u>loves</u> to be a
> part of the parade.

> **PR**
> Dana <u>is organizing</u> a talent show
> **P**
> at her school. She <u>invited</u> her brother
> **P**
> to emcee the event. She <u>asked</u> five of
> her teachers to judge the show. Now
> **PR**
> she <u>is getting</u> her friends to sign up
> for different acts. So far, people
> **P**
> <u>have signed up</u> for three singing acts,
> one comedy performance, and two
> **F**
> dancing routines. There <u>will be</u> more
> sign-ups before the night of the show.
> Audience and performers alike
> **F**
> <u>will have</u> a great time at the show!

Page 32

Answers will vary, but should follow the stated rules.

Page 33

1. rode—irregular
2. hit—irregular
3. ducked—regular
4. spied—regular
5. bought—irregular
6. ran—irregular
7. stood—irregular
8. fanned—regular
9. cried—regular
10. traded—regular
11. looked—regular
12. told—irregular
13. tracked—regular
14. tried—regular

Page 34

is, will find, nicknamed, will go, broke, hit, appear, held, stand, will be, is

Page 36

1. herself—reflexive
2. She—subject
3. It—subject
4. I—subject
5. us—object
6. He—subject
7. him—object
8. We—subject
9. us—object
10. himself—reflexive
11. themselves—reflexive

Page 37

1. I
2. We
3. They, us
4. He and I
5. myself
6. We
7. me
8. It
9. I, my
10. me
11. She and I
12. her

Page 38

1. themselves
2. They
3. he
4. His
5. ourselves
6. she
7. their
8. We
9. I
10. her
11. us
12. them

Page 40

Indefinite pronouns should be written in this order:

> Everybody
> No one
> few
> Many OR Several
> anything
> Everything
> Both

Page 41

1. interrogative
2. indefinite
3. indefinite
4. demonstrative
5. interrogative
6. indefinite
7. demonstrative
8. indefinite
9. indefinite
10. interrogative
11. demonstrative

Page 42

These words should be underlined:

What, Which, Anyone, These, everyone, everyone

Indefinite Pronouns
> Anyone
> everyone
> everyone

Page 42 (continued)
Demonstrative Pronouns
    These

Interrogative Pronouns
    What
    Which

Page 44
1. They ——▶ Cathy, friends
2. He ——▶ dad
3. She ——▶ Cathy
   them ——▶ tent, sleeping bag
4. he ——▶ dad
5. them ——▶ friends
6. it ——▶ bug spray
7. They, they ——▶ Cathy, dad

1. she OR her
2. he OR him
3. they OR them
4. it
5. they OR them
6. we
7. us
8. they OR them

Page 45
1. He
2. She, him
3. He, her
4. He, her, his
5. He, them
6. His
7. He, it

Page 46
He, He, his, he, He, it,
he, They, he, he, Its, he, They

Page 48
These words should be underlined,
with apostrophes added as indicated:
1. My
2. Grandma's
3. Mom's, Dad's
4. My, his
5. Children's
6. players'
7. My, bees', geese's

Page 48 (continued)
8. his
9. Darla's
10. Women's
11. park's
12. Wonderstads'

Page 49
1. <u>Zach's</u> birthday piñata was filled with (candies.)
2. <u>Karla's</u> stick hit the piñata first.
3. Next, <u>John's</u> stick hit the piñata.
4. The piñata finally broke with a hit from <u>Zach's</u> stick.
5. Birthday (candies) flew everywhere!
6. <u>Zach's</u> birthday (guests) picked up the (candies.)
7. <u>Zach's</u> (neighbors) came to join in the fun.
8. Even the (dogs) from down the street made their way to <u>Zach's</u> backyard.
9. The birthday (guests,) (neighbors,) and (dogs) all had a great time.
10. The <u>afternoon's</u> game was a big hit.
11. Zach can't wait to go to all of his (friends') birthday (parties) next!

Page 50
1. week's
2. weeks'
3. girl's
4. girls'
5. dollars
6. dollars'
7. lady's
8. ladies'
9. feet's
10. feet
11. church's
12. churches

Page 52
These words should be circled:

determined, every, beautiful, deadly,
bubonic, frightening, pesky, ugly,
foul, rats', food, Many, large, Busy,
their, crowded, Concerned, smelly,
household, airtight, metal, City, sewer,
School, their, dirt, their, meat, seven,
city, outdoor, their, city, clean, two
million, happy, free, horrible, bubonic

Page 53
Answers will vary.
1. This
2. those
3. that
4. Those OR These

Page 54
1. soccer ——▶ team
2. that ——▶ flavor
3. those, beautiful ——▶ landscapes
4. Two, full ——▶ truckloads
5. My, favorite ——▶ soup
   clam ——▶ chowder
   oyster ——▶ crackers
6. football ——▶ game
   this ——▶ Sunday
7. That ——▶ friend
   two ——▶ tickets
8. My, favorite ——▶ aunt
   long, white ——▶ veil
   her ——▶ wedding
9. many, fast, handsome ——▶ cars
10. three ——▶ pages
   hard ——▶ homework
   this ——▶ morning
11. two, difficult ——▶ songs
12. small, friendly ——▶ town

Page 56
1. most frightening—superlative
2. better—comparative
3. oldest—superlative
4. least likely—superlative
5. shorter—comparative
6. less active—comparative
7. most exciting—superlative
8. happier—comparative
9. hardest—superlative
10. more fun—comparative

Page 57
1. most wonderful S
2. faster C
3. most beautiful S
4. more fun C
5. more graceful C
6. youngest S
7. smaller C
8. more athletic C
9. busier C
10. most expensive S

Page 58
Sentences will vary, but should contain the following words:
1. pretty, prettier, prettiest
2. loud, louder, loudest
3. soft, softer, softest
4. careful, more careful, most careful
5. bad, worse, worst

Page 60
1. hard—how
2. late—when
3. everywhere—where
4. feverishly—how
5. early—when
6. loudly—how
7. clearly—how
8. frequently—when
9. wisely—how
10. often—when
11. very—to what extent
12. exceptionally—to what extent

Page 61
1. more carefully
2. better
3. worse
4. more quickly
5. more sweetly
6. most politely
7. most often
8. more noisily

Page 62
1. verb
2. verb
3. adverb
4. verb
5. adjective
6. verb

Page 62 (continued)
7. adjective
8. verb
9. verb
10. adverb
11. verb

1. adjective
2. adverb
3. adjective
4. adverb

Page 64
Answers may include the following:
1. at the park
2. behind the counter
3. After school
4. in the front
5. of cake
6. under the bridge
7. across the street
8. for breakfast
9. during summer vacation
10. of the tree
11. down the hill
12. from my big brother

Page 65
Sentences will vary.
1. <u>in</u> the end
2. <u>through</u> the back gate
3. <u>from</u> you
4. <u>into</u> the end zone
5. <u>to</u> my grandmother's house
6. <u>around</u> the world

Page 66
Mendoza is an important city in western Argentina. It sits at the foot of the Andes Mountains. A highway and a railroad both cross the Andes from Mendoza into Chile. Much of the wine and fruit produced in Argentina comes from Mendoza. Mendoza is also home to two large universities.

Page 66 (continued)
Santiago is the capital city of Chile. It is also the cultural center of Chile. There are many universities, cathedrals, zoos, government buildings, and museums in the city. Tourism is important to Santiago's economy. Over the years, Santiago has survived the destructiveness of earthquakes, floods, and civil unrest. Today, it is a popular city to visit.

Honduras is home to the city of Puerto Cortés. Puerto Cortés lies in northwestern Honduras. It was established in 1525. Bananas and coffee are shipped around the world from this port city. The economy of Puerto Cortés relies on manufactured and traded goods.

Page 68
1. of the contest—adjective
2. after breakfast—adverb
3. along the Missouri River—adverb
4. under the back porch—adverb
5. with red stripes—adjective
6. in one swallow—adverb
7. in the lemonade—adjective
8. before dinner—adverb
9. with great care—adverb
10. in my garden—adverb

Page 69
Answers will vary, but should contain adjectival phrases.

Page 70
1. in the morning—when
2. on Saturdays—when
3. for thirty-five minutes—how long
4. In the barn—where
5. for an hour—how long
6. by e-mail—how
7. for fifty years—how long
8. in the pasture—where
9. about an hour—how long
10. After school—when

Page 72

1. Professional photographers take pictures of people, landscapes, historic landmarks, and important events.
2. They may work for the media, for a commercial firm, or for themselves.
3. Photographers may work in the arts, the sciences, or the social sciences.
4. No change
5. Because he was a media photographer during the 1930s, Walker Evans recorded scenes of the Great Depression.
6. Once a fashion photographer for Vogue magazine, Cecil Beaton also worked as the official photographer of the British royal family.
7. Edwin Land invented the clever, convenient Polaroid for his three-year-old daughter.
8. No change
9. No change
10. If you like to take pictures, you might consider becoming a professional photographer.

Page 73

1. Elaine read a long, intriguing novel last month.
2. It was the story of three boys and their father.
3. Because the boys and their father went camping, the story was set in the woods.
4. No change
5. No change
6. Marcy, Nancy, and Taylor all enjoyed the story.
7. Kimberly likes to listen to soft rock music.
8. She also likes country, pop, and hard rock tunes.
9. She likes the grand, majestic sound of classical music as well.
10. While she does chores around the house, Kimberly listens to music.
11. Listening to music somehow makes her work easier and more fun.

Page 74

Answers will vary, but should contain the suggested words or phrases and appropriate punctuation.

Page 76

Kevin, I didn't...
Yes, I'm meeting...
Well, do you...
Yes, as a matter of fact, I do...try their blueberry pie, Rhonda.
No, I have...
Okay, but next...
I promise you, Kevin,...
You won't regret it, Rhonda...Look, there's Gordon!
Wow, I haven't...
Hey, is that Micah? I hope so, because...
Well, it was nice to see you, Kevin.
Thanks! I will. See you later, Rhonda.

Page 77

Answers will vary. Commas should follow all introductory words.

Page 78

2. May I, Grandma, help you bake a cake?
   May I help you bake a cake, Grandma?
3. I think, Thomas, your fever has finally broken.
   I think your fever has finally broken, Thomas.
4. I never knew, Helen, that you attended Foothill Elementary School.
   I never knew that you attended Foothill Elementary School, Helen.
5. Please, Daniel, come in from the rain.
   Please come in from the rain, Daniel.
6. Imagine, Stanley, a world with no wars.
   Imagine a world with no wars, Stanley.

Page 80

1301 W. Quincy Street
Garrett, Indiana
August 12, 2009

Dear Grandma,

Thanks for inviting my friends and me to your house next week. Mary, Lisa, and I expect to arrive around 6:00 on Sunday night. We will leave home around 6:00 on Saturday morning. Mary will drive from Denver, Colorado, to Omaha, Nebraska. We'll find someplace to clean up, eat dinner, and sleep a few hours. We should be back on the road by 6:00 Sunday morning. Lisa will drive from Omaha to Garrett. Because we'll be arriving around suppertime, we'll bring fast food from Charlie's Burgers in Garrett to share with you.

Last time we spoke, you asked what we might like to do while vacationing in the Midwest. The following is a list of places we would like to visit:
Auburn Cord Duesenberg Museum
Sandusky's sand dunes
Cedar Point Amusement Park

Although we would like to go to all the places on the list, we really just want to spend time with you. Can't wait to see you!

Love,
Doris

Page 81

Planned Events of the Ninth Annual Young Writers' Conference
Dana College
Blair, Nebraska
February 2, 2009
8:30–9:30   Breakfast
9:30–10:30 Keynote Speaker—Terry Willard from Seattle, Washington
10:30–12:00 Choose one of the following writing sessions:
            Developing Characters with Linda Algar from Ontario, Canada
            Playful Poems with Thomas Timmer from Milwaukee, Wisconsin
            Who Done It? with Sherry

Page 81 (continued)

Hartley from Cove, Oregon
Setting the Scene with Jerry Brown from Pittsburgh, Pennsylvania

12:00–1:00	Lunch
1:00–2:30	Choose one of the following writing sessions:

Writing Nonfiction with Tyler Young from San Francisco, California

Newspaper Reporting with Duane Heffelfinger from Blair, Nebraska

Selling Script Ideas with Alfred Hurston from Los Angeles, California

Using Storyboards with Walter Disby from Riverton, Wyoming

2:30–5:00	Critical Review Sessions
5:00–6:00	Dinner
6:00–10:00	Viewing of Shakespearean play in Lincoln, Nebraska

Page 82

1. ,
2. Both blanks filled with ,
3. All blanks filled with :
4. first blank : all others ,
5. ,
6. First blank : all others ,
7. ,

Page 84

1. Mary Dyer, a Quaker, was killed in 1660 for living in Boston, a city that once prohibited Quaker residency.
2. The 1931 Nobel Peace Prize winner, Jane Addams, founded Hull House, a social service settlement in Chicago.
3. Dorothy Day, an author, established "hospitality houses" for Great Depression victims during the 1930s.
4. Aesop's Fables, animal-based stories with morals, are the most widely read fables in the world.
5. A book of the teachings of Confucius, Lun Yü, has influenced both Eastern and Western thinkers.
6. The Hippocratic Oath, an oath written by the Greek physician

Page 84 (continued)

Hippocrates, continues to be used in the medical field today.

7. Andorra, a country located in southwestern Europe, covers 181 square miles.
8. A group of ten islands southwest of Africa, the Cape Verde Islands, are volcanic in origin.
9. Kiribati, formally the Gilbert Islands, is comprised of 33 islands in the west-central Pacific Ocean.
10. Mauritania, rich in iron ore and poor in plants and animals, is located in the Sahara Desert.

Page 85

The following should be circled:

my sister's school, Tamara White, the president of a local college, "Life on the Outside"

Martin Elliott, student body president, Tamara

the principal, White, a good friend of my sister

Page 86

Answers will vary, but should use appositives correctly.

Page 88

1. Tom asked, "Did you write this story, Jim?"
2. "Yes," Jim replied. "It was an assignment for English class."
3. "It is a very good story, Jim," Tom said. "Do you mind if I share it with my friends?"
4. While smiling shyly, Jim stammered, "That would be fine, Tom."
5. "Would you like to come to my birthday party, Shelly?" asked Katie.
6. "That would be fun," Shelly responded. "What would you like as a gift?"
7. "I like arts and crafts supplies," Katie replied.
8. "Then I know just the gift for you!" Shelly exclaimed.
9. "Where have you been?" complained Jacob. "We have all been waiting for you!"

Page 88 (continued)

10. "I had to take care of my little brother," Tyler explained.
11. "Oh, I forgot about that!" Nelson said. "I was supposed to tell you that before, Jacob. I'm sorry I forgot to relay your message, Tyler."
12. "That's okay," said Tyler. "I'm here now, so let's start the movie."

Page 89

1. "Mom, when does the dinner party start?" asked Larry.
2. "That was the best movie I've ever seen!" exclaimed Marcus.
3. Before the big test, my teacher reminded us, "Erase your first choice completely if you decide to change your answer."
4. "Marty said she would be here by three o'clock," Cecil reported.
5. Royal said, "I like to play volleyball."
6. The whole team chanted, "We are the champions! We are the champions!"
7. "Have you ever been to this restaurant before, Tiasha?" Cindy asked.
8. "You will get a good grade on today's test," I told myself.

Page 90

1. No changes
2. Mrs. Fields reminded me, "You don't have to get a perfect score; you just have to do your best."
3. Candy explained, "I was named after my aunt, not after a food!"
4. No change
5. No change
6. No change
7. "This is an excellent CD!" Anthony proclaimed.
8. No change
9. Mom told me, "Don't tell Dad what we got him for Christmas."
10. No change

Page 92

1. The book entitled Three by Finney by Jack Finney includes the stories "The Woodrow Wilson Dime," "Marion's Wall," and "The Night People."

Page 92 (continued)

2. "Moonlight Bay," a song written in 1912, was written by Edward Madden and Percy Wenrich.
3. This month's edition of <u>Stellar Students</u> magazine contains an excellent article entitled "Test-Taking Tricks."
4. My local newspaper is called <u>The Fairfield Press</u>.
5. The Shel Silverstein book <u>Where the Sidewalk Ends</u> contains a poem entitled "Where the Sidewalk Ends."
6. Last weekend, I attended a play called <u>Johnny Came Marching Home</u>.

Page 93

1. Rita watched the movie <u>Honey, I Shrunk the Kids</u> for the fourth time last night.
2. My class sang "By the Light of the Silvery Moon" for Grandparents' Day.
3. "Nicki's New Neighbor" is my favorite story in our literature book, <u>Stories from Around the World and Right Next Door</u>.
4. Sarah's essay, "Why We Have to Learn Math," was well researched.
5. During career day, a reporter from <u>The Market Valley Press</u> shared his latest story, "Teens and Teaching," with our class.
6. I wrote a poem entitled "Mine," which will be included in our school's literary journal, <u>Panther Pride</u>.

Page 94

Answers will vary, but titles should be punctuated correctly.

Page 96

1. I didn't bring any lunch money to school today.
2. My brother and I like to play football together.
3. Anthony and I are best friends.
4. They don't think they can make it to class today.
5. They've been waiting longer, so serve them first.
6. The postmaster gave the package to Mom and me.

Page 96 (continued)

1. incorrect
2. correct
3. correct
4. incorrect
5. incorrect

Page 97

1. I
2. them
3. them
4. am not
5. any
6. me
7. They
8. any
9. them
10. I
11. They
12. any, them

Page 98

Answers will vary, but they must use the given word correctly.

Page 100

The following sentences should be rewritten as indicated:

2. May I have an ice-cream cone?
4. Please sit down at your desk and begin your work.
5. If Randy sits on top of that counter, he will break it.
11. Ted also plays pretty well.
12. Who's your teacher this year?
14. Whose cat keeps coming to our front door?

Page 101

1. may
2. Lay OR Set
3. well
4. Whose
5. can
6. lie OR sit
7. Who's
8. sit
9. good
10. set OR lay

Page 102

1. who's
2. good
3. set
4. can
5. may
6. lay
7. well
8. lie
9. Whose
10. sits

Grammar and Punctuation Review Answer Key

A1.	C	B1.	A
A2.	A	B2.	C
A3.	A	B3.	C
A4.	B	B4.	B
A5.	C	B5.	B
A6.	C	B6.	A
A7.	B	B7.	A
A8.	B	B8.	B
A9.	B	B9.	C
A10.	A	B10.	A
A11.	B	B11.	C
A12.	A	B12.	A
A13.	C	B13.	B
A14.	A	B14.	C
A15.	B	B15.	B
A16.	A	B16.	B

Daily Language Review

Grades 1–8

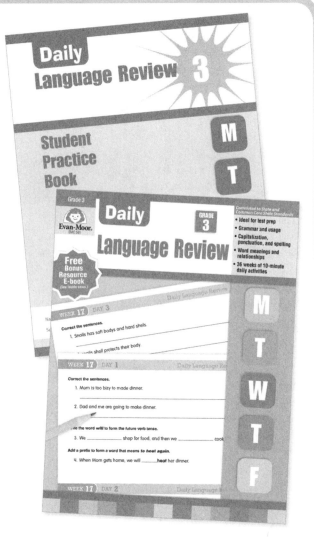

Proven effective in *improving* students' *language skills!*

Students practice grammar, punctuation, usage, and sentence-editing skills using the research-based model of frequent, focused practice.

- Students complete half-page activities on days 1–4 and a more extensive full-page activity on day 5.

- Includes a detailed scope and sequence, skills list, and home–school connection projects.

136 pages. Correlated to current standards.

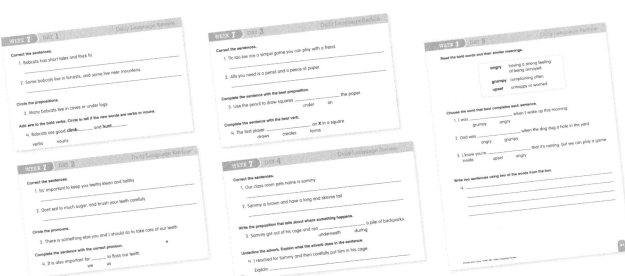

Daily Fundamentals: Morning Work

Grades 1–6

Give your students a **boost** with *Daily Fundamentals*!

Full-page daily activities provide practice using language, math, and reading comprehension skills, focusing on one skill in each subject area.

Each week of daily lessons progresses in difficulty as students move through Day 1 to Day 5, and the 30 weekly units progress in difficulty throughout the year.

With a detailed scope and sequence, you will always know the skills that your students are practicing and see where students need additional practice.

You can use *Daily Fundamentals* for morning work, bell ringers, homework, and informal assessment.

Correlated to current standards.

INCLUDES LANGUAGE, MATH, AND READING

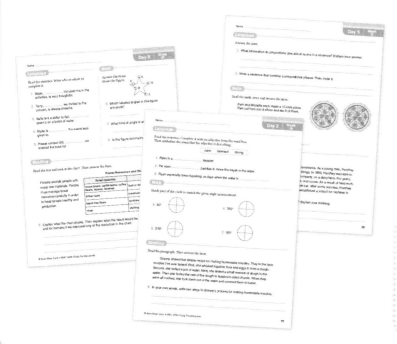

Teacher's Edition*		Student Pack (5 Student Books)	
Grade 1	EMC 3241	Grade 1	EMC 6331
Grade 2	EMC 3242	Grade 2	EMC 6332
Grade 3	EMC 3243	Grade 3	EMC 6333
Grade 4	EMC 3244	Grade 4	EMC 6334
Grade 5	EMC 3245	Grade 5	EMC 6335
Grade 6	EMC 3246	Grade 6	EMC 6336

*Available in print and e-book

Better Together

Complements the skill practice in:

- *Language Fundamentals*
- *Math Fundamentals*
- *Reading Comprehension Fundamentals*

A WORD A DAY

GRADES 1–6

Help *your students develop the* **rich and diverse** *vocabulary they need for* **academic success!**

Research shows that strong vocabulary and word knowledge is directly linked to academic accomplishment. Make sure your students develop the rich vocabulary that's essential to successful reading comprehension and academic achievement with *A Word a Day*.

Each book in this newly revised series covers 144 words in 36 engaging weekly units. And with new features, such as an oral review and a written assessment for each week, it's easier than ever to help your students develop the vocabulary they need.

Correlated to current standards.

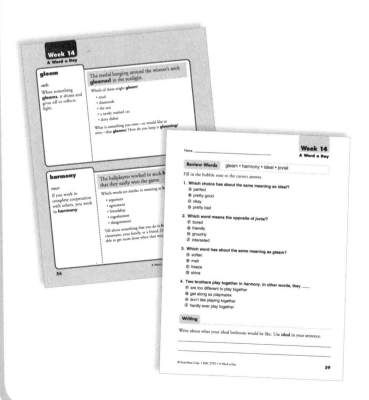

Teacher's Edition*		Student Pack (5 Student Books)	
Grade 1	EMC 2791	**Grade 1**	EMC 6611
Grade 2	EMC 2792	**Grade 2**	EMC 6612
Grade 3	EMC 2793	**Grade 3**	EMC 6613
Grade 4	EMC 2794	**Grade 4**	EMC 6614
Grade 5	EMC 2795	**Grade 5**	EMC 6615
Grade 6	EMC 2796	**Grade 6**	EMC 6616

*Available in print and e-book